80 recipes

for your...

Bread
maker

80 recipes
for your...
Bread
maker

Richard Ehrlich

Photography by Will Heap

Kyle Cathie Ltd

First published in Great Britain in 2011 by
Kyle Cathie Limited
23 Howland Street, London W1T 4AY
general.enquiries@kyle-cathie.com
www.kylecathie.com

10 9 8 7 6 5 4 3 2 1

ISBN 978-1-85626-943-8

Text © 2011 Richard Ehrlich
Photographs © 2011 Will Heap
Book design © 2011 Kyle Cathie Limited

Project editor: Catharine Robertson
Photographer: Will Heap
Designer: Mark Latter/www.bluedragonfly-uk.com
Food stylist: Annie Rigg
Props stylist: Sue Rowlands
Copy editor: Jan Cutler
Indexer: Alex Corrin
Production: Gemma John

A Cataloguing in Publication record for this title
is available from the British Library.

Printed and bound by Toppan Leefung Printing Ltd in China

contents

the rise of the machines

Bread made in a bread machine can be excellent – at least as good as, and sometimes better than, store-bought loaves. And some of the things I've made in the machine are largely indistinguishable from something made by hand.

If this surprises you somewhat, it positively astonishes me. For years I was a bread machine sceptic. The loaves I'd eaten and baked in the machines were nothing more than OK; some were pretty depressing. I also bristled at the idea, expressed by many able-bodied people of my acquaintance, that they 'don't have time' to bake bread by hand. Anyone who bakes by hand knows that it takes very little time – as little as 20 minutes of active work. These people were really saying: 'I want to be able to say I bake my own bread, but I'd rather spend my free time playing tennis.' I'm all in favour of tennis, but it shouldn't be used as an excuse for not baking bread.

Two things have changed since the days of my earlier scepticism. One: I learned that some people are physically unable to do the hard work of kneading. Old age, arthritis, carpal tunnel syndrome, general infirmity – all of these may make kneading impossible. Parents of very young children, whose time is so severely straitened, are another group for whom the hand-work is impractical. For these people, the bread machine is a godsend. Two: the machines seem to have improved. The first one that I used was made a good 15 or 20 years ago, and it just didn't do the trick. Those loaves had an unsatisfactory texture, close and dense, and the buckets – the part that holds the dough – had a peculiar shape that produced bread resembling no loaf I had ever seen.

In the spanking-new machines I've used in testing recipes for this book, the crumb is very good. The crusts, while not 100 per cent awesome, are more than satisfactory. And the shape of the finished loaf closely resembles that of 'real' bread. So, I am a convert to the machine-made loaf. If you need, or simply want, to have home-produced bread without the work of hand kneading, a bread machine is your ticket.

I should add, however, that I also hope that using the machine will inspire you to investigate the handmade loaf. Once you've done your share of baking using the machine's programs, try kneading in the machine and then letting it rise independently for timed baking. (There's a recipe on page 86.) Then try kneading in the machine, forming the loaf by hand, and baking in the oven. (See recipes on pages 86–103.) And maybe sometime soon you will try your hand at the handmade loaf. There are few better or more satisfying creations of the home kitchen. And no bread made in a bread machine will ever match the best handmade loaf baked by an experienced baker.

But you may just want to stick with the machine. And if that's the case, I'm with you.

some tips

buying: shape up
If you are contemplating the purchase of a bread machine, look for a model whose bucket gives a long loaf that closely resembles that of a standard loaf. Some buckets are deep, with short sides, and they produce bread with something like a pillar shape. This is the kind of loaf that made me hate bread machines initially. Avoid.

first step: master the manual
The very first thing you need to do with your bread machine is sit down with a cup of coffee (tea or water also allowed) and read the instruction manual from cover to cover. You should regard your manual as the first chapter of this book.

Pay special attention to the table – if there is one – that gives the times at which the different stages of production take place. You will need to refer to this again in all likelihood, but make its acquaintance right at the start.

measuring up
You need very little equipment apart from your machine, but it is essential that you possess the means to measure accurately by both weight and volume. For weighing, electronic scales that measure in increments of 5g – and preferably 2g – are the only type to have. They are not expensive. The best type is one with a flat platform on which you can put your bread-machine bucket or mixing bowl.

The other essentials are measuring spoons and jugs. If the manufacturer of your machine supplied these, use them. If not, buy from a good cookshop. Measuring vessels are sometimes inaccurate when shoddily manufactured, and you need absolute accuracy here. The jugs and spoons made by Oxo/Good Grips are excellent.

the right order
Every bread machine tells you to deposit the ingredients in a particular order. Follow the instructions, but note: the most important thing is to ensure that the yeast and water are separated by the flour. This is crucial regardless of whether you are baking immediately or setting the machine to bake with a time delay. If you are using the delay, however, it is vital: contact between the water and the yeast will make the yeast start working prematurely.

In my recipes, the ingredients are listed in an order that worked fine for me – and which also conforms generally to the principles laid out by most manufacturers. You can use my order rather than refer to the manual every single time you bake. But please note: if you use my order rather than the manufacturer's, the publishers and I cannot be held legally responsible.

crucial ingredients

There isn't much you need specifically for baking in the bread machine, except for fast-acting yeast. This may go by different names, but it is the only kind you can use in the machine because everything is designed to happen fast. Apart from the yeast you mainly need flours, several of them. I have tried to keep the number of flours to a minimum. Those I use here (in approximate order of importance) are:

strong white bread flour
This is flour that has a high gluten (protein) content, which is essential to enable the bread to expand during rising and baking.

strong wholemeal bread flour
The wholemeal equivalent, ground from the whole wheat grain including bran and germ. Wholemeal flour doesn't rise quite as well as white flour, which is why many recipes (including many in this book) combine it with white flour.

self-raising flour
This is plain flour with baking powder and sometimes bicarbonate of soda, both leaveners which enable the flour to rise. It doesn't rise as much as it would with yeast, but it's perfect for cakes and certain breads. Self-raising flour is usually white, but a brown variety is available.

plain flour
Flour with a lower gluten content, suitable for cakes.

rye flour
This is an exceptionally flavourful flour but it does not rise well. Always use in combination with wheat flour.

seeded flour
White or wholemeal flour with a combination of seeds, e.g. pumpkin, poppy, sunflower or sesame. You can make your own by adding seeds of your choice, around 10–15g per 100g of flour.

cornmeal
Ground maize kernels, used in cornbread and some conventional loaves.

semolina
A coarse, very hard flour made from durum wheat (the type used to make pasta). Semolina should be used sparingly in bread, but it gives a good firm texture to the loaf.

gluten-free flour
Flour containing no wheat, and therefore suitable for people with coeliac disease or severe gluten intolerance. Commercial gluten-free blends contain a combination of flours, including rice, potato, tapioca, maize and buckwheat.

getting into a scrape

Once your machine starts kneading, keep an eye on things for the first few minutes to make sure the kneading paddle is getting all the floury bits off the sides of the bucket. If it isn't, use a hand tool to scrape down the sides of the bucket. The tool can be plastic, silicone or wood – not metal, as that may scratch the bucket's non-stick coating. Sometimes it's necessary, sometimes it isn't.

a few minor adjustments

There's another reason to keep an eye on things in the early stages of kneading. Sometimes, for reasons I do not understand, even a well tested recipe needs a little adjustment: as it kneads in the machine, you can see that it is too wet or dry. If you watch for the first fifteen minutes or so of kneading, you'll see whether there's a problem. Dough looks gloopy? Add 50g of flour. Too stiff? Two tablespoons of water. That's the most you ever need, in my experience.

brushing up

You will get a much better texture in the crust if you brush the loaf just before baking with beaten egg, butter or extra virgin olive oil. This should be done before you put on any toppings you're planning to use.

Note: if you are using beaten egg, make sure the egg is beaten very well – until frothy and quite liquid. Under-beaten egg contains long strands of egg white which make it impossible to brush evenly.

lying in wait

Once you've switched the machine on, done any necessary scraping of the bowl, and added a second wave of ingredients after the bread has finished its initial kneading phase, you can pretty much go off and do whatever you want for two or three hours. The bread machine will complete its work all on its own. But there are two points at which you need to intervene. One is when the ping goes off to signal that it's time to add raisins or other 'bits' to the bucket (though note some bread machines have a raisin dispenser which adds 'bits' automatically.) The other is when the loaf is finished. You must be on hand to remove the bucket as soon as possible after baking is finished. Most machines have a 'keep warm' function that's intended to keep the bread in good condition once baking is done. In my experience, leaving it in the machine browns the sides too deeply and gives a soggy upper crust. Be ready for your bread when your bread is ready for you.

the clean-up

The non-stick lining in my bread machine rarely gets dirty enough to need full cleaning – a quick wipe with a damp cloth suffices, sometimes supplemented by a scrape with a fingernail to take off spots of stuck-on crust. If you want to wash more thoroughly, do it with detergent and water and brush. The bucket shouldn't go into the dishwasher, or come into contact with abrasive cleaners of any kind.

the paddle problem

In some machines, apparently, it is difficult detaching the paddle from the bucket after baking is finished. In others (mine included), you encounter the opposite problem: the paddle gets stuck in the finished loaf. Having a piece of metal inside a loaf of bread isn't exactly life-enhancing, but neither is it worth crying about. You can extract the paddle with a little knife-and-finger work, and 90 per cent of the slices look perfect. As the paddle is non-stick, you must take care when removing it with a knife. Use a round-tipped table knife and always hold it so that the cutting edge is cutting into the loaf rather than the paddle. A stout plastic knife is even better. You can also avoid the problem altogether by taking the paddle out of the bucket once kneading is complete and the dough is beginning its rise. You will become familiar with your machine's schedule very quickly and will know when to pull the paddle out. When you do this, you are left with just a shallow circular hole at the base of the loaf.

getting creative

The more you get to know your machine, the more you will see that standard operating procedures can be tweaked. Or even bent right out of shape. One of the most useful modifications I've discovered overcomes an apparently major shortcoming of the bread machine. In my own bread-making, I've long noticed (and I'm by no means the first) that a long, slow rise improves the flavour of the loaf. In standard bread machine recipes – including all of those in this book – the whole operation is complete in a few hours or even less. That means the rising of the dough is very speedy, with some loss of the flavour you get from a slow rise. If you use any of these recipes but cut the yeast in half, you can then use the kneading program on its own, leave the dough to rise more slowly, then do the baking with the Bake program a few hours later. The flavour is better, even if the process takes longer. It's worth trying. Unless, of course, you are desperate for a loaf.

salt

My recipes specify the amount of salt you should use. On the whole, these are in line with other bread machine recipes. If you prefer a less salty loaf, you can cut those quantities by 50 per cent and still get good results.

looks aren't everything

Sometimes a loaf comes out of the breadmaker with cosmetic imperfections: there's a hole in the interior that's too big; the top sinks a bit; the upper portion of the crumb separates from the crust; one end rises higher than the other. I don't know why it happens, and I don't care. I want my home-baked bread to taste good, not look like something from a professional bakery. And that should be your priority too.

simple breads

These are the bread-and-butter breads of this book, if you will pardon the expression. They are bread machining at its most basic, and I suppose they are where you should start if you are a novice. But simple doesn't have to mean boring. Adding a little something extra in the form of herbs or spices turns a simple bread into a special bread. And note: most of these can be used for sandwiches, regardless of whether they contain extra ingredients.

Fran Warde is a distinguished food writer who loves her bread machine. She says of this loaf: 'it's the only time that the kids get white bread as I will not buy it!' The relatively large quantity of yeast gives a light, airy loaf.

fran warde's white bread

225ml water
400g strong white bread
  flour
2 tablespoons vegetable
  oil
1½ teaspoons salt
2 tablespoons sugar
2 teaspoons fast-acting
  yeast
milk for brushing

Place the ingredients in the bucket following the order given in your manufacturer's instructions, or in the order listed here. Set the machine for the Basic setting and small/medium loaf size, and set the Crust/Colour setting for medium. Brush the top of the loaf with the milk just before baking begins. Turn the loaf out onto a wire rack as soon as possible after baking is complete.

Fran says: 'I remove it as soon as it is cooked and wrap it in a damp tea towel, making the loaf soft on the outside.'

She adds: 'I also use this recipe with brown flour, Granary, a dash of semolina added, with olive oil instead of vegetable and am often found adding seeds, much to my boys' annoyance!'

In my experience, you can add about 2 tablespoons of bran (wheat or oat) to most white loaves without adjusting any other ingredient or affecting the result. Add it along with the flour. This boosts the fibre content of the loaf – and even fussy children won't know it's there.

Soda bread is usually made with buttermilk, and you can use that if you can get hold of it. But my combination of milk and yoghurt works very well. This makes a loaf that's considerably lighter and airier than the standard soda bread – which is just the way I like it. Good with eggs or smoked fish.

soda bread

150ml yoghurt
150ml milk
150g strong wholemeal
   bread flour
75g self-raising flour
2 tablespoons oat bran
1 teaspoon salt
1 teaspoon bicarbonate
   of soda

Mix all the ingredients in a mixing bowl and spoon into the bucket. Bake using the Bake setting for 50 minutes, then test it by sticking a skewer into the centre; if the skewer comes out dry and hot, the bread is done. If not, cook for a further 10 minutes, checking again after 5 minutes. Turn the loaf out onto a wire rack as soon as possible after baking is complete.

Southern-style cornbread is one of greatest pleasures of the domestic kitchen – rich and luxurious as an accompaniment for fried chicken, braised meat or fishy stews. Some cooks put much more butter in than I do, but my version is rich enough. And using less butter means you can eat an extra slice as a reward for your restraint.

cornbread

250g medium or coarse cornmeal
75g self-raising flour
1½ teaspoons baking powder
½ teaspoon salt
325ml milk
100g softened butter, cut up into small pieces
1 egg, beaten

Mix all the ingredients in a bowl, then pour into the bucket and smooth the top as well as you can. Bake using the Bake setting for 60 minutes. Turn the loaf out onto a wire rack as soon as possible after baking is complete. Serve warm.

There are lots of variations on cornbread, some of them very good. The cheesy cornbread on page 50 is one example. Other good additions to the basic recipe include dried herbs (especially thyme), finely chopped chives or spring onions, or even just a generous grinding of black pepper.

Rye bread is one of the world's greats, but you have to take care with it: rye flour doesn't rise particularly well. The proportions here give plenty of rye flavour while still letting the loaf expand as it should. This is a good all-purpose loaf for sandwiches, cured fish, or German and Eastern European cold cuts.

rye bread

250ml water
50g butter
225g strong white bread flour
50g strong wholemeal bread flour
100g rye flour
1 teaspoon salt
2 teaspoons caraway seeds plus extra (optional) for sprinkling on top
1¼ teaspoons fast-acting yeast

Put the ingredients in the bucket following the order given in your manufacturer's instructions, or in the order listed here. Set the machine for the Basic setting and small loaf size, and the Crust/Colour setting for medium. Any time after the final kneading is finished, you can sprinkle caraway seeds on top; some people also spray the top with water to give extra sheen to the glaze. Turn the loaf out onto a wire rack as soon as possible after baking is complete.

Rye bread tastes better the more rye flour you put in it. If this loaf works well for you, try making it again with 175g of strong white bread flour and 150g of rye flour. It won't rise quite so well, but the flavour will be great.

Sourdough bread has become fashionable in recent years, with the rise of artisanal bakeries that include it in their lists. In some places, of course, it has never gone out of fashion: San Francisco sourdough is a well-established style now imitated elsewhere. And the breads of Pain Poilâne, expensive but memorable, are widely available in upmarket food shops. I've got a pair of machine-made adaptations that give a good idea of what the fuss is all about.

sourdough
introduction

Sourdough bread, made without yeast, is considered by some to be the apex of bread making. Maybe it is, maybe it isn't. I do think that a good sourdough loaf is about as good as bread ever gets, but wherever the truth lies, two things have become clear to me in my exploits with the bread machine. One: making the leaven for sourdough isn't nearly as terrifying as it is sometimes made out to be. Two: while bread machine manufacturers sometimes try to tell you that only fast-acting yeast can be used in their machines, sourdough can also be used.

My introduction to sourdough came through Andrew Whitley's *Bread Matters: The State of Modern Bread and a Definitive Guide to Baking Your Own*, a truly distinguished book, which gives the easiest method I have seen for making the leaven from which sourdough bread originates. I reproduce his method here, then give a couple of recipes for making the bread in the bread machine. The initial stages may look complicated, but they are actually very simple. You just put some flour and water in a bowl and mix them together. You do the same thing for three more days. By that time, in theory, the leaven (which is what you have just made) is ready to be used as the basis for a loaf of sourdough bread.

One technical note is needed. Andrew Whitley recommends keeping the starter as close as possible to a consistent temperature of 28°C. This is difficult to maintain, but putting the bowl next to a sunny window or a radiator (in cold weather) should do the trick. If necessary, you can also get it started at a warm temperature by heating the bowl in the microwave for 20 seconds or so. You may need to move the bowl around, but it's worth the trouble.

Carrying on with sourdough

Once your leaven is established, you can keep it alive more or less indefinitely by feeding it fresh water and flour once a day. You can do this by eye as long as you never put in more than half the quantity of leaven. If you're not that dedicated, however, the leaven left over from the main recipe here will be enough to bake another two or three small loaves.

Sourdough Starter

Like many, if not most, professional bakers, Whitley gives measurements for water in weight. I have followed his practice here.

First Day
40g strong wholemeal bread flour
40g water

Mix the flour and water in a large bowl and cover tightly.

Second Day
40g strong wholemeal bread flour
40g water

Mix the flour and water with the existing starter and cover tightly.

Third Day
40g strong wholemeal bread flour
20g water

Mix the flour and water with the existing starter and cover tightly.

Fourth Day
120g strong white bread flour
100g water

Mix the flour and water with the existing starter and cover tightly. Your starter will be ready to use the next day.

This has a fairly dense texture which I think suits the tangy sourdough flavour. For a lighter texture, use equal quantities of sourdough and strong white bread flour.

sourdough wholemeal

250g sourdough starter
225ml water
75g strong white bread
flour
225g strong wholemeal
bread flour
2 tablespoons oat bran
(optional)
1 teaspoon salt
melted butter or oil, for
brushing

Put all the ingredients in the bucket following the order given in your manufacturer's instructions, or in the order listed here. Set the machine for the Knead/ Dough setting. When the kneading cycle is over, take out the paddle carefully and leave the dough to rise until it has roughly doubled in size. Brush the top with melted butter or oil and bake using the Bake setting for 1 hour. Turn the loaf out onto a wire rack as soon as possible after baking is complete.

This produces a flavourful bread with a fairly firm texture. Excellent sliced thinly, toasted or grilled, and eaten with pâté or strong cheeses.

sourdough semolina

150ml water
125g sourdough starter
100g strong bread flour
200g medium semolina
1 teaspoon salt

Put all the ingredients in the bucket following the order given in your manufacturer's instructions, or in the order listed here. Set the machine for the Knead/ Dough setting. When the dough is ready, leave it to rise to roughly double its size; this may take 2 or 3 hours in warm weather but can be double that if the weather is cold.

Brush the top with melted butter if you wish, and set the machine to Bake for 1 hour 10 minutes. Turn the loaf out onto a wire rack as soon as possible after baking is complete.

My daughter Rebecca can't eat yeast for medical reasons, and misses out on good bread when she can't get sourdough or soda bread. I invented this as a savoury substitute for her. Note that it is made like a cake, from a stirred but unkneaded dough and using baking powder in place of yeast. When I made it for Rebecca, the other people who ate it thought it was great – and some didn't guess that it contained no yeast. You can vary the recipe by adding one to two tablespoons of bran for extra roughage.

rebecca's yeast-less white bread

150g self-raising flour
100g strong white bread flour
1¼ teaspoons baking powder
30ml vegetable oil
1 egg, lightly beaten
1 teaspoon sugar
1 teaspoon salt

Sift the flours and baking powder into a mixing bowl. Add all the remaining ingredients and beat thoroughly with a spoon just until well blended. Spoon into the bucket and bake using the Bake setting for 1 hour. Turn the loaf out onto a wire rack as soon as possible after baking is complete.

Buckwheat is not often used in bread because it doesn't rise well. But it has a wonderful flavour, as you know if you have ever eaten blini, Russian yeasted pancakes. Here's a bread that gets a little of the inimitable buckwheat taste but still rises well. This is good with smoked fish, or with fish roe, sour cream and chives – the standard partners for blini.

buckwheat bread

300g strong white bread flour
75g strong wholemeal bread flour
75g buckwheat flour
1 tablespoon vegetable oil
50g butter
1¼ teaspoons salt
1¼ teaspoons fast-acting yeast

Put all the ingredients in the bucket following the order given in your manufacturer's instructions, or in the order listed here. Set the machine for the Basic setting and medium loaf size, and the Crust/Colour setting for medium. Turn the loaf out onto a wire rack as soon as possible after baking is complete.

Yellow because of eggs and turmeric, which gives a lovely colour.
Note: this recipe differs from others in this book in employing less
yeast than would normally be used and a manual rise after the Knead/
Dough program. If you want to use the fully automatic method, use
twice the amount of yeast and the Basic setting on your machine.

the yellow loaf

125ml water

3 eggs

50g strong wholemeal
bread flour

350g strong white bread
flour

25g butter, cut into small
pieces

2 teaspoons clear honey

½ teaspoon turmeric

½ teaspoon salt

½ teaspoon fast-acting
yeast

melted butter or oil, for
brushing

coarse salt (optional), for
sprinkling on top

Put the ingredients in the bucket following the order
given in your manufacturer's instructions, or in the order
listed here. Set the machine for Knead/Dough. When the
kneading cycle is over, take out the paddle carefully and
leave the dough to rise until it is roughly doubled in size.

Brush the top with butter or oil and bake using the
Bake setting for 1 hour. You could also sprinkle some
coarse salt on top before baking. Turn the loaf out onto
a wire rack as soon as possible after baking is complete.

The loaf in the picture shows the kind of cosmetic
imperfection – in this case, a teardrop-shaped air bubble
– that sometimes occurs in bread making. Don't ask
me why. It's one of life's little mysteries. And don't worry
about it. You're looking for good taste, not
visual perfection.

Oatmeal is used here to give good texture to a
basic loaf combining white and wholemeal flour.
This is wonderful at breakfast with butter and jam,
and is also a good sandwich loaf.

oatmeal bread

225ml water
50g oatmeal
100g strong wholemeal
   bread flour
200g strong white bread
   flour
25g oat bran
1 tablespoon clear honey
1 teaspoon salt
1¼ teaspoons fast-acting
   yeast

Put all the ingredients in the bucket following the order
given in your manufacturer's instructions, or in the order
listed here. Set the machine for the Basic setting and
medium loaf size, and set the Crust/Colour setting for
medium. Turn the loaf out onto a wire rack as soon as
possible after baking is complete.

If you wish, you can add extra flavour by using treacle
or molasses instead of the honey.

This is the great celebration bread of Eastern European Jewry. Poppy seeds sprinkled on top make a good addition. Eat toasted or untoasted with eggs, soft cheese, cream cheese or as a sandwich loaf. Or use it to make French toast, for which it is perfectly suited.

challah

125ml water
375g strong white bread
    flour
25g oat bran
50g sugar
3 eggs
1 teaspoon fast-acting
    yeast
1 teaspoon salt

Put all the ingredients in the bucket following the order given in your manufacturer's instructions, or in the order listed here. Set the machine for the Basic setting and small/medium loaf size, and set the Crust/Colour setting for medium. Turn the loaf out onto a wire rack as soon as possible after baking is complete.

This recipe is based on one in a lovely book called *The Melting Pot: Balkan Food and Cookery*, by Maria Kaneva-Johnson. The loaf is sweet and dense, perfect for a weekend brunch.

wholemeal honey bread

200ml milk
250g strong wholemeal
    flour
100g strong white bread
    flour
2 tablespoons vegetable
    oil
5 tablespoons clear honey
½ teaspoon salt
1 teaspoon fast-acting
    yeast
50g walnuts, finely
    chopped

Put all the ingredients, except the walnuts, in the bucket following the order given in your manufacturer's instructions, or in the order listed here. Set the machine for the Basic/Raisin setting and medium loaf size, and set the Crust/Colour setting for medium. When the ping for adding ingredients goes off, or halfway through kneading, add the walnuts. Turn the loaf out onto a wire rack as soon as possible after baking is complete.

This is inspired by a recipe in *Bread: From Ciabatta to Rye*, by my bread-baking hero Linda Collister. Linda uses white flour and rye, but the denser texture of strong wholemeal bread flour suits me. Use a brew with good flavour and preferably a dark colour.

beer bread

330ml beer, ale or stout
50g rye flour
100g strong white bread flour
300g strong wholemeal bread flour
2 tablespoons malt extract
¼ teaspoon ground cloves
1½ teaspoons salt
1¼ teaspoons fast-acting yeast

Put all the ingredients in the bucket following the order given in your manufacturer's instructions, or in the order listed here. Set the machine for the Wholemeal setting and medium loaf size, and set the Crust/Colour setting for medium. Turn the loaf out onto a wire rack as soon as possible after baking is complete.

I loved raisin bread when I was young, and this rich loaf brings those memories back. Toasted, and spread while piping-hot with good butter, it is one of the all-time great teatime treats. It's also good with cream cheese.

raisin bread

100g raisins
400ml water
500g strong white bread flour
50g strong wholemeal bread flour
50g brown sugar
50g butter, cut in pieces
2 eggs
½ teaspoon salt
1¼ teaspoons fast-acting yeast
1 teaspoon ground cinnamon
beaten egg, for brushing

Soak 25g of the raisins in hot water for about 10 minutes. Drain the soaked raisins and put with the other raisins in a bowl.

Put all the ingredients, except the raisins, cinnamon and beaten egg, in the bucket following the order given in your manufacturer's instructions, or in the order listed here. Set the machine for the Basic/Raisin setting and for the medium loaf size, and set the Crust/Colour setting for medium. When the ping for adding ingredients goes off, or halfway through kneading, add the raisins and cinnamon. Brush the top of the loaf with the egg just before baking begins. Turn the loaf out onto a wire rack as soon as possible after baking is complete.

Soaking the raisins isn't a necessity, but the contrast in textures is nice – and some of the softened raisins get mashed up during kneading and thus spread throughout the loaf. Note: this recipe is not as sweet as some. Add an extra 25g of sugar, if you wish.

Sometimes I like to make a side starch dish spicy rather than the main dish it's accompanying. This is an example, which would go well with simply-cooked fish, chicken or vegetables. It's also good with sandwiches containing something relatively bland and (toasted) with creamy dips.

spiced bread

200ml water
250g strong white bread flour
3 cardamom pods, split and seeds removed
½ teaspoon each of freshly ground black pepper, ground cumin and ground coriander
¼ teaspoon ground cinnamon
2 tablespoons extra virgin olive oil
1¼ teaspoons fast-acting yeast

Put all the ingredients in the bucket following the order given in your manufacturer's instructions, or in the order listed here. Set the machine for the Basic setting and medium loaf size, and the Crust/Colour setting for medium. Turn the loaf out onto a wire rack as soon as possible after baking is complete.

If you like, you can use whole cumin and coriander seeds, and grind the pepper very coarsely, to get more texture and crunch. You can also use half milk and half water, and butter instead of the extra virgin olive oil.

This has a nicely springy and delicate crumb, with the spices lending oomph. It is more of a breakfast bread than the one on the facing page. Serve with yoghurt and/or fruit.

sweet spicy bread

275ml milk
375g strong white bread
  flour
50g butter, cut up into
  small pieces
1 egg
¼ teaspoon ground
  cloves
½ teaspoon ground
  allspice
1 teaspoon ground
  ginger
1 teaspoon ground
  cinnamon
¼ teaspoon grated
  nutmeg
4 tablespoons brown
  sugar
1 teaspoon fast-acting
  yeast

Put all the ingredients in the bucket following the order given in your manufacturer's instructions, or in the order listed here. Set the machine for the Basic setting and medium loaf size, and set the Crust/Colour setting for medium. Turn the loaf out onto a wire rack as soon as possible after baking is complete.

This is a very tasty bread but not one you would want to eat every day. It's a good candidate, therefore, for freezing. Slice what you want to freeze and freeze the slices individually on a baking sheet, then transfer to a plastic bag. Freezing them separately ensures that they will not stick together in the bag.

I made this when I had some leftover dried figs and was very pleased with the result. The figs lend a touch of sweetness and crunch, plus that inimitable dried-fruit flavour. Combined with the seeds and grains they give a good chewy texture which makes this an ideal breakfast bread with butter or yoghurt.

seeded fig bread

300ml water
200g strong white bread flour
100g strong wholemeal bread flour
100g seed and grain flour
4 tablespoons vegetable oil
1¼ teaspoons fast-acting yeast
1 teaspoon salt
4 dried figs, finely chopped
beaten egg or melted butter, for brushing

Put all the ingredients, except the figs, in the bucket following the order given in your manufacturer's instructions, or in the order listed here. Set the machine for the Basic/Raisin setting and medium loaf size, and set the Crust/Colour setting for medium or high. When the ping for adding ingredients goes off, or halfway through kneading, add the figs. Brush the top of the loaf with the egg or butter just before baking begins. When baking is complete, leave for 10 minutes, then turn the loaf out onto a wire rack.

This bread has a lovely texture, soft and dense at the same time, and the dill gives it a nice lift. I got the idea from a recipe in Paul Hollywood's *100 Great Breads*, but my method differs from his in using mashed potato.

potato and dill bread

1 small baking potato,
about 125g in weight
350ml milk
400g strong white
bread flour
50g butter
1 teaspoon salt
1 teaspoon dill seed
12–15 fresh dill sprigs,
finely chopped
1 plump garlic clove,
finely chopped
1 teaspoon fast-acting
yeast
melted butter, for
brushing

Peel the potato and slice it thinly. Put it in a small pan with salted water to cover, bring to the boil, then turn down the heat and simmer for 15 minutes or until just cooked. Drain off the water and mash, then leave to cool completely.

Put all the ingredients in the bucket following the order given in your manufacturer's instructions, or in the order listed here, adding the potatoes after the flour. Set the machine for the Basic setting and medium loaf size, and set the Crust/Colour setting for medium or high. Brush with butter just before baking begins. Turn the loaf out onto a wire rack as soon as possible after baking is complete.

If you want to do something closer to the original recipe, chop the potatoes into small chunks instead of slices. Cook in the water until barely done, then set the machine to Basic/Raisin and add them when the ping goes off, or halfway through kneading.

This isn't proper brioche, one of the glories of French baking, but it has the hallmark egginess and sweetness. An excellent loaf for teatime, or as a base for fresh berries with whipped cream, thick yoghurt or fromage blanc. Toasted, it would go well with a creamy, buttery chicken liver parfait.

brioche loaf

150ml milk
300g strong white bread
    flour
3 eggs
50g sugar
75g butter, melted
½ teaspoon salt
1¼ teaspoons fast-acting
    yeast
melted butter, for
    brushing

Put the milk, flour, eggs, sugar and butter in the bucket, followed by the salt and yeast. Use the Knead/Dough setting. When it is complete, remove the kneading paddle and close the lid. Let the dough rise to roughly twice its size (about 1 hour).

Brush with the melted butter and bake for 30–40 minutes, until the top is lightly browned and the loaf sounds hollow when rapped with your knuckles.

Brioche makes really good breadcrumbs for both sweet and savoury dishes. If you have some left over, slice it and leave it to dry completely on a wire rack. Process in a food processor, or break it up using a kitchen mallet or an empty wine bottle.

flavoured breads

There's almost nothing – within reason – that you can't use to add variety and fun to basic bread. And I hope you will come up with your own inventions. Just one word of caution. As soon as you introduce 'foreign' ingredients into bread, you are adding an extra element of unpredictability. No two onions, peanut butters, pestos, etc., are exactly alike. So with the breads in this chapter, it's worth paying careful attention during kneading, and adding either flour or water as you think appropriate. These breads are especially prone to sinking, which affects appearance but never flavour.

Plain or toasted, this would make a nice summer lunch with a great big mixed salad. To get a very strong goat's cheese flavour, use a cheese that's had some ageing rather than one of the softer young cheeses. And you could also add a large pinch of dried thyme, a herb that has a particular affinity with goat's cheese.

goat's cheese and sun-dried tomato bread

300ml water
450g strong white
   bread flour
2 tablespoon extra
   virgin olive oil
4 sun-dried tomatoes
   (about 50g in weight),
   finely chopped
1 teaspoon salt
1 teaspoon fast-acting
   yeast
100g crumbly goat's
   cheese, broken up into
   small pieces

Put all the ingredients in the bucket following the order given in your manufacturer's instructions, or in the order listed here. Set the machine for the Basic setting and small/medium loaf size, and set the Crust/Colour setting for medium. Turn the loaf out onto a wire rack as soon as possible after baking is complete.

This is really tasty stuff. I have made it here using the manual method, with a small amount of yeast relative to the quantity of flour so that the dough rises slowly, allowing the flavours to develop. If you want to do it automatically, double the yeast, use the Basic setting, and set the loaf size to medium.

onion and garlic bread

2 plump garlic cloves, finely chopped
1 small onion, finely chopped
60ml vegetable oil or melted butter
300ml water
500g strong white bread flour
1 teaspoon cumin seeds
1 teaspoon salt
½ teaspoon fast-acting yeast
melted butter, for brushing (optional)

Gently cook the garlic and onion in 1 tablespoon of the oil or butter until they're fragrant and lightly coloured (about 5 minutes). Leave to cool to room temperature.

Put all the ingredients in the bucket following the order given in your manufacturer's instructions, or in the order listed here. Set the machine for the Knead/Dough setting. When the dough is ready, carefully remove the paddle and leave the dough to rise to roughly double its size; this should take 1–3 hours, depending on the temperature in your kitchen. Brush the top with melted butter if you wish, and set the machine to Bake for 1 hour. Turn the loaf out onto a wire rack as soon as possible after baking is complete.

You can vary the spices in this loaf: coriander, caraway and dill seed would all be good. And you can use more of the spices for a stronger, more pungent flavour.

A simple but exceptionally tasty loaf, good for sandwiches. Soft Italian cheeses such as Fontina go well with fennel, as does chicken in any guise. Just make sure you cut out the woody core from the fennel before chopping and adding to the mix – it sometimes stays annoyingly crunchy even after cooking.

fennel and red onion bread

250ml water
1 tablespoon extra virgin olive oil
375g strong white bread flour
1 teaspoon salt
1 teaspoon fast-acting yeast
1 small fennel bulb (about 100g in weight), finely chopped
1 small red onion (around 100g in weight), finely chopped
extra virgin olive oil, for brushing

Put all the ingredients, except the fennel and onion, in the bucket following the order given in your manufacturer's instructions, or in the order listed. Set the machine for the Basic/Raisin setting and small/medium loaf size, and set the Crust/Colour setting for medium. When the ping for adding ingredients goes off, or halfway through kneading, add the fennel and onion. Brush the top of the loaf with the oil just before baking begins. Turn the loaf out onto a wire rack as soon as possible after baking is complete.

A great accompaniment for scrambled eggs, cooked with a bit of chopped parsley or coriander, if you like. If you're a real chilli fiend, you can eat the eggs with a pickled pepper for extra kick. Note that some cooks in the American south, where this kind of loaf was first made, would use far more chillies than I have used here. If you want to emulate them, fire away – but up to a maximum of ten chillies, because more than that might make the loaf too wet. And by the way, you can use small fresh chillies if you can't find pickled jalapeños where you do your shopping. You can also use another fairly sharp cheese if you have no Cheddar.

cheesy cornbread with jalapeño chillies

250g medium or coarse cornmeal
75g self-raising flour
1½ teaspoons baking powder
½ teaspoon salt
325ml milk
50g softened butter, cut into small pieces
50g grated Cheddar cheese
1 egg, beaten
1 or 2 pickled jalapeño chillies, finely chopped

Mix all the ingredients in a bowl, then pour into the bucket and smooth the top as well as you can. Cook using the Bake setting for 1 hour. Lift the bucket out of the machine, but leave the loaf in the bucket for 10 minutes, then turn out carefully onto a wire rack. Turn the bread over, and leave for at least 5 minutes before slicing. Serve warm.

GSG is the acronym I use for ginger, spring onion and garlic, the holy trinity of Chinese cookery. I worship the trinity in all its guises, including this unusual and very distinctive bread.

gsg bread

200ml water
1 teaspoon salt
275g strong white bread flour
1 teaspoon fast-acting yeast
1 tablespoon vegetable oil
1 teaspoon sesame oil
1 egg
1 thick slice fresh ginger, peeled and finely chopped
1 plump garlic clove, finely chopped
1 large or 2 small spring onions, finely chopped
beaten egg, for brushing

Put all the ingredients, except the ginger, garlic and spring onions, in the bucket following the order given in your manufacturer's instructions, or in the order listed here. Set the machine for the Basic/Raisin setting and small/medium loaf size, and the Crust/Colour setting for medium or high. When the ping for adding ingredients goes off, or halfway through kneading, add the ginger, garlic and spring onions. Brush the top of the loaf with the egg just before baking begins. Turn the loaf out onto a wire rack as soon as possible after baking is complete.

This is a variation of Rebecca's Yeast-less White Bread (page 26). An illustration – and a tasty one at that – of one way a basic recipe can be altered with extra flavourings.

rebecca's garlic and olive bread

150g self-raising flour
100g strong white bread flour
1¼ tablespoons baking powder
1 garlic clove, finely chopped
1 small red or green chilli, finely chopped
50g butter, melted
1 egg, beaten
1 teaspoon salt
5 large green olives, pitted and coarsely chopped
extra virgin olive oil, for brushing

Sift the flours and baking powder into a mixing bowl. Add all the remaining ingredients, except the olives, and beat thoroughly with a spoon just until well blended. Spoon into the bucket and scatter the olives on top, pressing them into the batter so that most are submerged. Brush the top with the oil and bake using the Bake setting for 1 hour. Turn the loaf out onto a wire rack as soon as possible after baking is complete.

You could also use good streaky bacon, and another sharp, hard cheese such as Pecorino. But pancetta and Parmesan really are best. This is a strongly-flavoured bread that could almost be a meal in itself with a few slices of avocado and a slice of creamy cheese.

pancetta and parmesan bread

75g pancetta or good bacon, rind removed and cut into shreds
200ml water
325g strong white bread flour
1 tablespoon vegetable oil
1 egg
½ teaspoon salt
1 teaspoon fast-acting yeast
25g grated Parmesan
3–4 sage leaves, each cut into 3 or 4 pieces
beaten egg, for brushing

Put the pancetta or bacon in a small non-stick frying pan with a little dash of vegetable oil, if it is very lean. Cook over a low heat (with regular stirring) for 5 minutes or until it is lightly browned. Leave to cool.

Put the water, flour, oil, egg, salt and yeast in the bucket following the order given in your manufacturer's instructions, or in the order listed here. Set the machine for the Basic/Raisin setting and small/medium loaf size, and the Crust/Colour setting for medium. When the ping for adding ingredients goes off, or halfway through kneading, add the pancetta, cheese and sage. Brush the top of the loaf with the egg just before baking begins. Lift the bucket out of the machine, but leave the loaf in the bucket for 10 minutes, then turn the loaf out onto a wire rack.

The cornmeal adds a nice bit of firm crunch to the texture here. For more flavour, add a crushed clove of garlic. The only trick is to watch during the first minutes of kneading, because some commercial pestos are more oily than others. If the dough seems too dry, add a couple of spoonfuls of water. If too wet, add a little flour. This bread would go very well with a plate of Italian cheeses and cold cuts for a weekend lunch, or with roasted or barbecued vegetables.

pesto and cornmeal bread

200ml water
250g strong white bread flour
2 teaspoons fine cornmeal
1 tablespoon extra virgin olive oil
2 tablespoons pesto
1 teaspoon salt
1 teaspoon freshly ground black pepper
1 teaspoon fast-acting yeast
melted butter or oil, for brushing
coarse salt (optional), for sprinkling on top

Put the ingredients in the bucket following the order given in your manufacturer's instructions, or in the order listed here. Set the machine for the Basic setting and medium loaf size, and the Crust/Colour setting for medium. Brush the top with butter or oil just before baking begins. You could also sprinkle some coarse salt on top at the same time. Turn the loaf out onto a wire rack as soon as possible after baking is complete.

This is almost a meal in itself when served with a green salad, but scrambled or poached eggs would complete the picture very nicely.

mediterranean bread

350ml water
2 tablespoons extra virgin olive oil
2 tablespoons tomato purée
450g strong white bread flour
½ teaspoon salt
½ teaspoon dried oregano
1 teaspoon fast-acting yeast
4 anchovy fillets, coarsely chopped
1 roasted red pepper, deseeded, peeled and coarsely chopped

Put the water, oil, tomato purée, flour, salt, oregano and yeast in the bucket following the order given in your manufacturer's instructions, or in the order listed here. Set the machine for the Basic/Raisin setting and medium loaf size, and the Crust/Colour setting for medium. When the ping for adding ingredients goes off, or halfway through kneading, add the anchovies and peppers. Turn the loaf out onto a wire rack as soon as possible after baking is complete.

If you don't like anchovies – and there are plenty of people who don't – you can still make this bread by substituting 1 tablespoon capers. It won't taste the same, but it will be good.

This recipe was inspired by one in Paul Hollywood's *100 Great Breads*, a wonderful book. This would make a good base for scrambled eggs, or for sautéed vegetables such as mushrooms or peppers. If you can't find ricotta, a mild goat's cheese would make an even tangier substitute. Cottage cheese would also be usable, but you will have to watch the dough while it's kneading because cottage cheese is more watery than ricotta. Add up to 50g flour if necessary.

ricotta and chive bread

250ml water
375g strong white bread
  flour
25g oat bran
150g ricotta cheese
1 teaspoon salt
½ teaspoon freshly
  ground black pepper
4 tablespoons extra
  virgin olive oil
1 teaspoon fast-acting
  yeast
10–12 chives, finely
  chopped
melted butter or extra
  virgin olive oil, for
  brushing
coarse salt or finely
  chopped chives
  (optional), for
  sprinkling on top

Put all the ingredients in the bucket following the order given in your manufacturer's instructions, or in the order listed here. Set the machine for the Basic setting and small/medium loaf size, and set the Crust/Colour setting for medium or high. Brush the top with butter or oil just before baking begins; you could also sprinkle some coarse salt or finely chopped chives on top at the same time. Turn the loaf out onto a wire rack as soon as possible after baking is complete.

This is a good partner for Spanish charcuterie, such as Serrano ham or chorizo. Good without toasting, but even better with it. And this is also a good bread to use for making Pan con Tomate (pa amb tomàquet), the ubiquitous Catalan standby.

saffron and paprika bread

large pinch of saffron
  threads, crumbled
175ml water
375g strong white bread
  flour
1 teaspoon paprika or
  Spanish pimentón
2 teaspoons coarsely
  ground black pepper
25g butter or
  2 tablespoons extra
  virgin olive oil, plus
  extra for brushing
1 teaspoon fast-acting
  yeast
coarse salt (optional), for
  sprinkling on top

Put the saffron in a small bowl and gently heat 50ml of the water, then pour over the saffron and leave for 10 minutes. (You can do this easily in the microwave by heating at full power for 20 seconds or so.)

Add the saffron water to the bucket followed by the other ingredients in the order given in your manufacturer's instructions, or in the order listed here. Set the machine for the Basic setting and medium loaf size, and the Crust/Colour setting for medium. Brush the top with butter or oil just before baking begins. You could also sprinkle some coarse salt on top at the same time. Turn the loaf out onto a wire rack as soon as possible after baking is complete.

pan con tomate

To make Pan con Tomate, rub the toasted bread with a peeled garlic clove so that the pulp gets scraped onto the bread. Now rub the bread with a halved tomato. Drizzle on as much extra virgin olive oil as you like, then sprinkle over a little coarse salt, and eat either on its own or as part of a cold lunch.

A nice summery loaf with a delicately moist crumb. Serve it alongside a seasonal salad, especially one with tomatoes and basil, and a good selection of cheeses. Note: using two small courgettes rather than one larger specimen is greatly preferred, because the larger ones can be more watery.

courgette and spring onion bread

200ml water
350g strong white bread flour
1 plump garlic clove, finely chopped
1 teaspoon salt
½ teaspoon freshly ground black pepper
2 tablespoons vegetable oil
1 teaspoon fast-acting yeast
2 small courgettes, about 200g total weight, coarsely grated
1 large or 2 small spring onions, finely chopped
melted butter, for brushing

Put all the ingredients, except the courgettes and spring onions, in the bucket following the order given in your manufacturer's instructions, or in the order listed here. Set the machine for the Basic/Raisin setting, the loaf size for small/medium, and the Crust/Colour setting for medium or high. When the ping for adding ingredients goes off, or halfway through kneading, add the courgettes and spring onion. Brush the top of the loaf with butter just before baking. Lift the bucket out of the machine, but leave the loaf in the bucket for 10 minutes, then turn the loaf out onto a wire rack.

The garlic idea comes from a recipe in *The Richard Corrigan Cookbook*, but is used in a completely different way from Corrigan's. If you want to tamp down the garlic flavour even further, simmer it for an extra ten or even twenty minutes. But the flavour isn't excessively strong when the cloves are given the cooking time here. This savoury bread is ample enough in flavour to serve as a side dish, but it's also good for sandwiches.

confit garlic bread

6 plump garlic cloves, peeled
50g butter
275ml water
375g strong white bread flour
25g oat bran
½ teaspoon fresh thyme
1 tablespoon balsamic vinegar
1 teaspoon salt
1 teaspoon fast-acting yeast
butter, for brushing
coarse salt or finely chopped thyme (optional), for sprinkling on top

Put the garlic and half the butter in a small pan with just enough water to cover. Bring to the boil, then turn down the heat and simmer for 10 minutes, or until the garlic is slightly softened and very fragrant. Turn off the heat and leave to cool to room temperature.

Put all the ingredients in the bucket following the order given in your manufacturer's instructions, or in the order listed here. Set the machine for the Basic setting and small/medium loaf size, and set the Crust/Colour setting for medium or high. Brush the top with butter just before baking begins; you could also sprinkle some coarse salt or finely chopped thyme on top at the same time. Turn the loaf out onto a wire rack as soon as possible after baking is complete.

Rice bread is a good way of using up leftovers, but it's tasty enough
– especially when made with basmati – to make it worth cooking
rice specially for it. If cooking the rice from scratch, use 50g.

basmati rice bread

250ml water
1 tablespoon vegetable oil
250g strong white bread
  flour
100g strong wholemeal
  bread flour
½ teaspoon black
  mustard seeds
½ teaspoon coriander
  seeds
1 teaspoon salt
1 teaspoon fast-acting
  yeast
100g cooked basmati rice
  or plain long-grain rice
  (50g raw weight)
melted butter, for
  brushing

Put all the ingredients, except the rice, in the bucket
following the order given in your manufacturer's
instructions, or in the order listed here. Set the machine
for the Basic/Raisin setting and small/medium loaf size,
and set the Crust/Colour setting for medium. When the
ping for adding ingredients goes off, or halfway through
kneading, add the rice. Brush the top of the loaf with the
butter just before baking begins. Turn the loaf out onto a
wire rack as soon as possible after baking is complete.

Note: never keep rice warm once it is cooked, as a
nasty food-poisoning bacterium called *bacillus cereus*
can develop. If you want to use cooked rice later, cool
it quickly then chill.

The flavours of the classic Russian soup in a surprising and delicious loaf. Great with smoked or cured fish – and it toasts well.

borscht bread

250ml water
475g strong white
  bread flour
1 medium onion, about
  75g, finely chopped
50g butter
1 teaspoon salt
1¼ teaspoon fast-acting
  yeast
1 small beetroot, about
  125g, peeled and
  coarsely grated
1 small baking potato,
  about 125g, peeled and
  coarsely grated
melted butter, for
  brushing

Put all the ingredients, except the beetroot and potato, in the bucket following the order given in your manufacturer's instructions, or in the order listed here. Set the machine for the Basic/Raisin setting and medium loaf size, and set the Crust/Colour setting for medium. When the ping for adding ingredients goes off, or halfway through kneading, add the beetroot and potato. Brush with butter just before baking begins. Turn the loaf out onto a wire rack as soon as possible after baking is complete. Cool for at least 10 minutes before slicing – if you can resist the temptation.

I use thyme for this, but rosemary or sage would be just as good. Makes a good companion for eggs, especially scrambled. You can use another cheese if you want, and this is a good way to play around with the basic recipe. As long as it's nothing soft, your choice should be dictated by your personal preference: Manchego, Parmesan, Pecorino, Caerphilly, etc.

cheesy bread with thyme

175ml water
250g strong white bread
  flour
1 teaspoon salt
a few good grindings of
  black pepper
50g butter, cut into small
  pieces
1¼ teaspoons fast-acting
  yeast
50g strong Cheddar
  cheese, cut into small
  pieces
1 teaspoon fresh thyme
  or ½ teaspoon dried
beaten egg, for brushing

Put all the ingredients, except the cheese and thyme, in the bucket following the order given in your manufacturer's instructions, or in the order listed here. Set the machine for the Basic/Raisin setting and small/medium loaf size, and set the Crust/Colour setting for medium or high. When the ping for adding ingredients goes off, or halfway through kneading, add the cheese and thyme. Brush the top of the loaf with the egg just before baking begins. When baking is complete, turn the loaf out onto a wire rack.

This is almost like the savoury equivalent of the carrot cake on page 115, but the effect is completely different. Sliced thinly, it makes a good accompaniment to dips and salads. Sliced more thickly, it is very good for sandwiches made with a mayonnaisey filling (chicken, egg, prawn, etc.).

carrot and coriander bread

250ml water
300g strong white bread flour
1 teaspoon salt
2 teaspoons fast-acting yeast
small handful fresh coriander, leaves only, finely chopped
2 small carrots (about 125g total weight), peeled and coarsely grated
melted butter, for brushing

Put all the ingredients, except the carrots, in the bucket following the order given in your manufacturer's instructions, or in the order listed here. Set the machine for the Basic/Raisin setting and small/medium loaf size, and set the Crust/Colour setting for medium. When the ping for adding ingredients goes off, or halfway through kneading, add the carrots. Brush the top of the loaf with the butter just before baking begins. Turn the loaf out onto a wire rack as soon as possible after baking is complete.

Carrot and coriander have a natural affinity, but parsley could be substituted if you wish. Chervil is another herb that likes carrots, and the finely chopped white part of a small spring onion would add a little extra zing.

This savoury, earthy bread is an excellent accompaniment to eggs and cured fish. The only trick is to watch during the first minutes of kneading, because some sweet potatoes are more watery than others. If the dough seems too dry, add a couple of spoonfuls of water. If too wet, add a little flour.

sweet potato bread

250ml water
225g strong white bread
  flour
150g strong wholemeal
  bread flour
1 teaspoon salt
½ teaspoon freshly
  ground black pepper
1 teaspoon vegetarian
  bouillon powder
225g cooked sweet
  potato, roughly
  chopped
50g butter
1 teaspoon fast-acting
  yeast
melted butter, for
  brushing

Put all the ingredients in the bucket following the order given in your manufacturer's instructions, or in the order listed here. Set the machine for the Basic setting and the loaf size for large, and set the Crust/Colour setting for medium. Brush the top of the loaf with the butter just before baking begins. Turn the loaf out onto a wire rack as soon as possible after baking is complete.

This is a really good breakfast bread with butter
and honey, but it's also good for sandwiches.

malted loaf with oat bran

350ml water
300g strong white bread
   flour
200g strong wholemeal
   bread flour
1 teaspoon salt
1 tablespoon malt extract
1 tablespoon clear honey
3 tablespoons oat bran
1¼ teaspoons fast-acting
   yeast

Put the ingredients in the bucket following the order given in your manufacturer's instructions, or in the order listed here. Set the machine for the Wholemeal setting and large loaf size, and set the Crust/Colour setting for medium or high. Turn the loaf out onto a wire rack as soon as possible after baking is complete.

A simple loaf given extra texture and a subtle flavour
by pinhead oatmeal and the tang of yoghurt.

oatmeal yoghurt bread

200ml milk
100ml low-fat plain
   yoghurt
100g strong wholemeal
   bread flour
300g strong white bread
   flour
75g pinhead oatmeal
1 tablespoon sugar
1 teaspoon salt
1 teaspoon fast-acting
   yeast

Put all the ingredients in the bucket following the order given in your manufacturer's instructions, or in the order listed here. Set the machine for the Basic setting and medium loaf size, and set the Crust/Colour setting for medium or high. Turn the loaf out onto a wire rack as soon as possible after baking is complete.

For this loaf, the bananas should be just ripe, or even a little under-ripe. This is a dense bread, like all those made with only strong wholemeal bread flour, but surprisingly light. A killer brunch toast with scrambled eggs.

banana bread
the savoury version

300ml milk
375g strong wholemeal
  bread flour
50g porridge oats
25g butter, cut into small
  pieces
1 tablespoon brown
  sugar
3 bananas, cut into small
  pieces
½ a small onion, finely
  chopped
1 teaspoon fast-acting
  yeast
1 teaspoon salt

Put all the ingredients in the bucket following the order given in your manufacturer's instructions, or in the order listed here. Set the machine for the Wholemeal setting and medium loaf size, and set the Crust/Colour setting for medium. Turn the loaf out onto a wire rack as soon as possible after baking is complete.

This is breakfast in a loaf – it even has an egg! All that's missing is a slice of bacon and a cup of coffee. Try to choose a muesli that isn't too heavy on the dried fruit, and watch during the first few minutes of kneading. If the dough seems too dry, add a couple of spoonfuls of water. If too wet, add a little flour.

muesli bread

225ml milk
250g strong white bread flour
150g strong wholemeal bread flour
50g butter, cut into small pieces
1 egg
2 tablespoons clear honey
1 teaspoon fast-acting yeast
100g muesli
1 teaspoon salt

Put all the ingredients, except the muesli, in the bucket following the order given in your manufacturer's instructions, or in the order listed here. Set the machine for the Basic/Raisin setting and medium loaf size, and set the Crust/Colour setting for medium. When the ping for adding ingredients goes off, or halfway through kneading, add the muesli. Turn the loaf out onto a wire rack as soon as possible after baking is complete. Cool for at least 10 minutes before slicing.

This is chewy, moist and quite complex in flavour from those different grains. It toasts very well and would make a respectable accompaniment to roast or barbecued meats.

multi-grain bread

350ml water
125g mixed seed and grain flour
100g strong white bread flour
75g rye flour
150g strong wholemeal bread flour
2 tablespoons vegetable oil
1 teaspoon salt
1 teaspoon fast-acting yeast
½ teaspoon dried mixed herbs (optional)

Put all the ingredients in the bucket following the order given in your manufacturer's instructions, or in the order listed here. Set the machine for the Basic setting and medium loaf size, and set the Crust/Colour setting for medium or high. Turn the loaf out onto a wire rack as soon as possible after baking is complete.

This tasty bread makes a good companion for Italian cold cuts. The only trick is to watch during the first minutes of kneading, because one semolina is never quite like another. If the dough seems too dry, add a couple of spoonfuls of water. If too wet, add a little flour.

herbed bread with pecorino

350ml water
100g strong wholemeal bread flour
300g strong white bread flour
50g fine semolina
3 tablespoons extra virgin olive oil
1 teaspoon fast-acting yeast
½ teaspoon dried sage
½ teaspoon dried oregano
½ teaspoon freshly ground black pepper
100g Pecorino Romano cheese, coarsely grated, plus extra for sprinkling on top
2 thick slices of onion, about 75g total weight, roughly chopped
beaten egg, for brushing

Put all the ingredients, except the cheese and onions, in the bucket following the order given in your manufacturer's instructions, or in the order listed here. Set the machine for the Basic/Raisin setting and set the Crust/Colour setting for medium. When the ping for adding ingredients goes off, or halfway through kneading, add the cheese and onion. Brush the top of the loaf with the egg and sprinkle with grated cheese just before baking begins. Turn the loaf out onto a wire rack as soon as possible after baking is complete.

All the flavours of the delicious dip in a loaf. The texture is dense, making this a good bread for slicing thinly and serving with dips.

hummus bread

300ml water
4 tablespoons extra
    virgin olive oil
325g strong white bread
    flour
1 teaspoon salt
2 tablespoons tahini
1 teaspoon ground
    cumin
small handful parsley,
    finely chopped
150g cooked chickpeas
extra virgin olive oil,
    for brushing

Put all the ingredients, except the chickpeas, in the bucket following the order given in your manufacturer's instructions, or in the order listed here. Set the machine for the Basic/Raisin setting and medium loaf size, and set the Crust/Colour setting for medium. When the ping for adding ingredients goes off, or halfway through kneading, add the chickpeas. Brush the top of the loaf with the oil just before baking begins. Turn the loaf out onto a wire rack as soon as possible after baking is complete.

Hummus is a dish that withstands any number of variations without collapsing under their weight, and some of them can be incorporated into this bread. Add a roughly chopped roasted pepper, well drained and well dried, along with the chickpeas. Boost the spice content with ½ teaspoon paprika and 1 teaspoon ground coriander. Or squeeze in a blob of tomato purée along with the initial ingredients.

This bread is inspired (duh!) by southern-style cornbread, but the effect is drier and less rich. And it serves a different purpose: this is a slicing loaf, good as a base for an open-top sandwich of meat or poultry, or as the enclosure for a burger.

rich corn loaf

350ml milk
175g cornmeal
225g strong white
  bread flour
75g sweetcorn kernels,
  canned or thawed
  frozen
1 egg
50g butter, cut into
  small pieces
1 teaspoon salt
1¼ teaspoons fast-acting
  yeast

Put all the ingredients in the bucket following the order given in your manufacturer's instructions, or in the order listed here. Set the machine for the Basic setting and medium loaf size, and set the Crust/Colour setting for medium or high. Turn the loaf out onto a wire rack as soon as possible after baking is complete.

Sweetcorn goes well with alliums (either plain onions or spring onions), so for extra pizzazz, add 1–2 tablespoons of either one (finely chopped).

A rich, chewy loaf that would love a good swipe with the butter knife followed by a generous layer of raspberry or strawberry jam. You could also use it as a sandwich bread. Peanut butter goes well with bacon, chicken and – as Elvis Presley discovered with calamitous consequences – mashed banana.

peanut butter bread

300ml milk
100g strong wholemeal
  bread flour
250g strong white bread
  flour
2 eggs
75g butter
100g chunky peanut butter
1 teaspoon fast-acting yeast
1 teaspoon salt
melted butter, for brushing
coarse salt or finely
  chopped peanuts
  (optional), for sprinkling
  on top

Put all the ingredients in the bucket following the order given in your manufacturer's instructions, or in the order listed here. Set the machine for the Basic setting and medium loaf size, and set the Crust/Colour setting for medium or high. Brush the top with butter just before baking begins; you could also sprinkle some coarse salt or finely chopped peanuts on top at the same time. Turn the loaf out onto a wire rack as soon as possible after baking is complete.

gluten-free

It is thought that around 1 per cent of the population suffers from coeliac disease, in which the immune system attacks the small intestine whenever it comes into contact with gluten. Sufferers have to avoid the principal bread flours, including wheat and rye.

It is possible to bake bread using gluten-free flours such as rice, potato, tapioca, maize and buckwheat. The bread machine, however, doesn't do the job to a quality level that satisfies me. There are two recipes here for gluten-free breads, and they are tasty. I haven't put in more than that because other books deal with handmade gluten-free breadmaking, and that's the way to do it. The books are *Bread Matters*, by Andrew Whitley, and *Seriously Good! Gluten-Free Baking*, by Phil Vickery.

If you avoid gluten because you think you are intolerant to it, I urge you to get the diagnosis confirmed by a doctor. Foregoing bread and cake (not to mention pasta, biscuits, and much more) deprives you of a lot of serious gastronomic pleasure. Make sure you really need to avoid gluten before taking this step.

The soft raisins open out the structure of the typically closed gluten-free crumb, and add variety to the texture as well as sweetness. Like any raisin bread, this is best used with butter and a cup of tea or milk on the side. It also improves with toasting.

gluten-free raisin bread

300ml water
425g gluten-free flour
2 tablespoons honey
50g golden granulated sugar
1 teaspoon salt
50g raisins
¼ teaspoon ground cloves
¼ teaspoon ground cinnamon
1¼ teaspoons fast-acting yeast

Put all the ingredients in the bucket following the order given in your manufacturer's instructions, or in the order listed here. Set the machine for the Fast/Rapid or Gluten-free setting and small/medium loaf size, and set the Crust/Colour setting for medium. When the program is finished, test the bread by sticking a skewer in the centre. If it doesn't come out dry and hot, bake for another 5 minutes. Turn the loaf out onto a wire rack as soon as possible after baking is complete.

Another example of how a generous dose of chopped ingredients improves the texture of a gluten-free loaf. This makes a good sandwich loaf for cheese or cold meats.

gluten-free onion bread

300ml water
350g gluten-free flour
150g onion, finely
   chopped
2 tablespoons oat bran
1 teaspoon salt
2 tablespoons extra
   virgin olive oil
1 ¼ teaspoons fast-acting
   yeast

Put all the ingredients in the bucket following the order given in your manufacturer's instructions, or in the order listed here. Set the machine for the Fast/Rapid or Gluten-free setting and small/medium loaf size, and set the Crust/Colour setting for medium. Turn the loaf out onto a wire rack as soon as possible after baking is complete.

kneaded breads

You don't need to bake breadmaker bread in the breadmaker alone. They all have a Knead/Dough setting which does nothing more than that, so you can do the hard work in the machine and then shape your dough into a different form for baking in the oven. I've included a handful of recipes here for that two-stage baking. It's worth the extra work: those different shapes are part of the joy of baking. And it's also worth keeping a supply of a good all-purpose dough in the fridge, covered tightly, for occasions when you're turning on the oven to cook something else and you feel like having a bit of bread to go with it. The all-purpose dough (page 86) and versatile dough (page 88) are both good candidates for this.

You can shape the dough to make one large loaf, two medium-sized loaves or eight rolls. It can also be used for pizza bases.

all-purpose bread dough

425ml water
675g strong bread
  flour (white or a
  combination of 500g
  white and 175g
  wholemeal), plus
  extra for dusting
1–2 teaspoons salt
2 teaspoons fast-acting
  yeast
2 tablespoons vegetable
  oil

Put all the ingredients, except the oil, in the bucket following the order given in your manufacturer's instructions, or in the order listed here. Set the machine to the Knead/Dough setting. Pour the oil into a large bowl.

When the dough is ready, remove it from the bucket and shape it into a ball. Put it in the bowl and turn it so that the whole ball is covered with oil. Cover the bowl with clingfilm and leave until the ball has roughly doubled in size. This can take anything from 1–3 hours, depending on the temperature in your kitchen. If it suits your schedule, you can slow down the rising by keeping the bowl in the fridge.

To make a loaf, knock back the dough and cut it in half. Shape into a lozenge that will fit into a small loaf tin and pat the dough into it. Leave to rise again until the dough has nearly reached the top of the tin. Preheat the oven to 200°C/180°C fan/Gas 6, and use a baking stone if you have one. Spray the top of the loaf with water and put a ramekin or similar dish full of water on the rack under which the loaf will be sitting. (The steam helps to achieve a good crust.) Put the loaf in the oven and bake for 30–35 minutes, or until the bread is nicely browned and feels hollow when you tap it with your knuckles. Cool the bread on a wire rack.

This began life as a variation on the pizza dough recipe in *Chez Panisse Pasta, Pizza & Calzone* by Alice Waters (of the renowned Chez Panisse in Berkeley, California) with Patricia Curtan and Martine Labro. I quickly discovered that it's good not just for pizza but for other quick breads, and this makes it a good candidate for a dough to keep on hand at all times. I've also made breadsticks, calzone and (of course) pizza from the same dough. This dough is a faster riser because of the quantity of yeast. Halve it and the dough will rise more slowly.

a versatile dough

175ml water
275g strong white
    bread flour
100g strong wholemeal
    bread flour
1 tablespoon milk
2 tablespoons extra
    virgin olive oil, plus
    extra for greasing
2 teaspoons fast-acting
    yeast

Put all the ingredients in the bucket following the order given in your manufacturer's instructions, or in the order listed here. Set the machine for the Knead/Dough setting. Turn out into a lightly oiled bowl, turn once to coat with oil, cover with cling film, and leave until it has roughly doubled in size.

This recipe makes one. You can make as many as you like as long as the pan is big enough – or cook them in batches.

griddled flatbreads

75g versatile dough
  (a lump about 5cm
  in diameter)
¼ teaspoon cumin
  seeds
flour, for dusting
around 1 teaspoon
  extra virgin olive oil
salt (optional), for
  sprinkling on top

Heat a stainless steel, cast iron or anodised aluminium griddle or heavy frying pan over a high heat. Roll or press the ball of dough into a circle about 12.5cm in diameter (or into an oval of roughly comparable size). Press the cumin seeds firmly into the dough on one side only. If you are making more than one flatbread, just leave each one on a lightly floured work surface while you make the rest.

Put the bread(s) in the pan with the unseeded side facing down. Cook until well browned underneath (about 4 minutes), and in the meantime, brush the top with the oil. (You can also sprinkle on some fine salt if you like, before brushing.) Turn and continue cooking until lightly browned underneath, 1–2 minutes. These can be served hot or at room temperature.

The famous Italian loaf takes many forms, all of them extremely popular when the loaf is well made. For this bread, as for any baked in the oven, placing the baking sheet on a baking stone will help you achieve a better crust on the base. Makes one loaf.

focaccia

150ml water
250g strong white bread flour
50g strong wholemeal bread flour
2 tablespoons extra virgin olive oil
1 teaspoon salt
1 teaspoon fast-acting yeast
olive oil and coarse salt, for sprinkling on top

Put all ingredients in the bucket following the order given in your manufacturer's instructions, or in the order listed here. Set the machine for the Knead/Dough setting. Lightly oil a bowl with vegetable oil while the dough is rising.

When the dough is ready, remove it from the bucket and shape it into a ball. Put it in the oiled bowl and turn it so that the whole ball is covered with oil. Cover the bowl with clingfilm and leave until the ball has roughly doubled in size. This can take anything from 1–3 hours, depending on the temperature in your kitchen. If it suits your schedule, you can slow down rising by keeping the bowl in the fridge.

To form the loaf: roll or press out the dough onto a lightly oiled baking pan to a thickness of around 2.5cm. Dimple the top all over with your fingertips, at intervals of around 5cm. Leave to rest for 30 minutes, covered.

Preheat the oven to 200°C/180°C fan/Gas 6, and use a baking stone if you happen to have one. Drizzle the bread with olive oil, sprinkle with coarse salt and bake until well browned (20–25 minutes).

Focaccia toppings

Fresh herbs, e.g. thyme, sage
   or rosemary
Coarsely ground black pepper
Garlic, finely chopped
Thinly sliced onions, raw or sautéed
   in oil until soft
Finely chopped anchovies
Sun-dried tomatoes, finely chopped
Green or black olives
Grated Parmesan or Pecorino

Potatoes and other starch get mixed together by Italian cooks in a number of forms and a number of areas. This bread is based on one that comes from a Tuscan baker by way of Carol Field's *Focaccia: Simple Breads from the Italian Oven*. The original is a schiacciata, a bread that's similar to focaccia. I have simplified by using the focaccia dough.

focaccia with potatoes and rosemary

1 quantity of focaccia dough (page 90)
100g new potatoes
about 75ml extra virgin olive oil, plus extra for greasing
6–8 sprigs fresh rosemary, finely chopped, or 1 teaspoon dried rosemary
coarse salt and freshly ground black pepper

After the dough has risen to double its size in the bowl, roll or press it out into a lightly oiled baking pan to a thickness of about 2.5cm. Dimple the top all over with your fingertips, at intervals of about 5cm. Leave to rest for 30 minutes, covered.

In the meantime, boil the potatoes until they are barely cooked – a knife should slide through to the centre easily (about 10 minutes). Drain, leave to cool, then slice very thinly.

Preheat the oven to 200°C/180°C fan/Gas 6, and use a baking stone if you happen to have one. Lightly drizzle the bread with the oil, then scatter on the potato slices and the rosemary. Sprinkle the bread with salt and plenty of freshly ground black pepper. Bake until well browned (about 20–25 minutes). Cool the focaccia on a wire rack. Serve at room temperature.

This is adapted from a recipe in *Sally Clarke's Book: Recipes from a Restaurant, Shop and Bakery.* Though not usually a fan of seeded breads, I like this one because the fleshy seeds (sunflower and pumpkin) are used in just the right amount. And the sprinkled seeds make for unusual complexity. A good all-purpose roll.

sally clarke's granary rolls with four seeds

300ml water
300g strong wholemeal bread flour
200g strong white bread flour, plus extra for dusting
1 tablespoon sunflower seeds
1 tablespoon pumpkin seeds
2 teaspoons salt
1½ teaspoons fast-acting yeast
1 teaspoon clear honey
oil, for greasing
1 teaspoon sesame seeds
1 teaspoon poppy seeds

Put all the ingredients, except the sesame and poppy seeds, in the bucket, following the order given in your manufacturer's instructions, or in the order listed here. Set the machine for the Knead/Dough setting. Turn out into a lightly oiled bowl, turn once to coat with oil, cover with cling film, and leave until it has roughly doubled in size. In the meantime, mix the sesame and poppy seeds in a small bowl.

Place the kneaded bread on a floured work surface and cut into twelve pieces. Shape into slightly elongated rolls, and roll each one in the mixed seeds – press the seeds in gently to make sure they stick. Place each roll on a non-stick or lightly oiled baking sheet, cover again, and leave to rise for 30 minutes or until they have risen by about 50 per cent.

Preheat the oven to 200°C/180°C fan/Gas 6. Put the baking sheet on the middle shelf and bake for 15 minutes or until the rolls are crisp and well browned, and sound hollow when tapped. Cool the bread on a wire rack.

These should be smallish – not as big as an ordinary dinner roll. Serve warm with butter or slice in half and dish out with apéritifs.

sesame cheese rolls

150g versatile dough
  (a lump about 7.5cm
  in diameter)
flour, for dusting
3–4 tablespoons grated
  hard cheese, such as
  Parmesan, pecorino or
  mature Cheddar cheese
freshly ground black
  pepper
oil, for greasing
about 2 teaspoons coarse
  salt
1 tablespoon sesame
  seeds

Roll the dough out into a piece about 10 x 15cm on a floured work surface. Sprinkle the cheese over it, then grind black pepper on lightly. Roll up the dough into a cylinder, then roll the cylinder on the table or between your hands until it's about 5cm in diameter. Cut into six to eight pieces and place them on a lightly oiled baking sheet. Cover loosely and leave for 30 minutes.

Preheat the oven to 200°C/180°C fan/Gas 6. Sprinkle salt and sesame seeds lightly over the rolls. Put the baking sheet on the middle shelf and bake for about 15 minutes or until the rolls are crisp and well browned, and sound hollow when tapped.

You don't have to use sesame seeds for this. The sprinkling could just as easily be of cumin, caraway, fennel or dill seeds. And a little parsley or chives in the mix would add yet another dimension of flavour.

The great Marcella Hazan writes: 'The recipes for pizza dough are beyond numbering', and she is right. There are two ways of dealing with this profusion of recipes. One is to find a recipe that you like and then stick with it. The other is never to make it the same way twice in a row, so you can play around and judge the differences wrought by changes in measurements.

pizza dough

150ml water
250g plain flour
2 tablespoons extra
   virgin olive oil, plus
   extra for greasing
1 teaspoon salt
1 teaspoon fast-acting
   yeast

Put all the ingredients in the bucket following the order given in your manufacturer's instructions, or in the order listed here. Set the machine for the Knead/Dough setting. Turn out into a lightly oiled bowl, turn once to coat with oil, cover with cling film, and leave until it has roughly doubled in size.

Toppings for pizza are almost infinite in variety. Here is one to get you started. Sautéing the mushrooms first makes them weep less liquid onto the pizza.

mushroom pizza with tomato sauce and pecorino

½ quantity of pizza
   dough
flour, for dusting
100g closed-cap white
   or brown mushrooms,
   thickly sliced
2 teaspoons vegetable oil
½ teaspoon dried
   rosemary
100ml good tomato
   sauce, preferably
   homemade
50g Pecorino Romano or
   Pecorino Sardo, shaved
   thinly and crumbled
   into small pieces
3 tablespoons extra
   virgin olive oil
freshly ground black
   pepper

Roll out the dough into a thin circle about 40cm in diameter. Lightly flour a thin metal baking sheet and put the dough on it.

Put the mushrooms in a non-stick frying pan with the vegetable oil and cook at a brisk heat until they're well coloured and reduced in thickness by about 50 per cent. Turn off the heat, sprinkle with the rosemary, and set aside.

Preheat the oven to 230°C/210°C fan/Gas 8. If you have a baking stone, put it in the oven now. Leave to preheat for at least 15 minutes. Using a small ladle or large spoon, spread the sauce out as evenly as possible over the base to within 2.5cm of the perimeter. Scatter the mushrooms all over, then sprinkle on the cheese. Finally, drizzle over the olive oil and grind over some black pepper. Slide the baking sheet onto the baking stone and bake for 20 minutes or until the topping is bubbling hot and the crust is crisp and risen. Serve immediately.

This is loosely modelled on the recipe for ensaïmadas, sweet bread rolls, which you'll find in Charmaine Solomon's *The Complete Asian Cookbook*. When I first made it I discovered that it's a surprisingly versatile preparation; note the variations at the end of the recipe. Note also: my way of rolling out the pastries is different (and simpler) than the original. Makes 50–60 puffs.

cheese puffs

125ml milk
375g plain flour, plus extra for dusting
2 eggs
100g softened butter, cut into small pieces
1 teaspoon salt
1 teaspoon fast-acting yeast
100g melted butter, for brushing
around 100g sharp, hard cheese such as mature Cheddar or Manchego
beaten egg, for brushing

Put the milk, flour, eggs and butter in the bucket, followed by the salt and yeast, or in the order given in your manufacturer's instructions. Set the machine for the Knead/Dough setting. When it is complete, remove the kneading paddle and close the lid. Let the dough rise to roughly twice its size (about 1 hour).

Carefully remove the dough to a floured work surface, handling it gently, as it is quite a soft and delicate substance. Flatten it gently, then cut into six even-sized pieces. Roll out one piece to a flat slab 20 x 25cm and 3mm thick. Brush it lightly with butter, then scatter cheese over in an even layer. Roll it up, starting from a short side. Roll out again to a thickness of 3mm and cut the slab into 7.5cm squares. Put the squares onto a greased baking sheet and repeat with all the remaining dough. You will need three or four baking sheets. Cover loosely and leave at room temperature for at least 30 minutes or chill and leave for as long as you like.

Preheat the oven to 220°C/200°C fan/Gas 7. Brush the squares with beaten egg. Bake until puffy and crisp, about 10-12 minutes.

variations

Roll out into small ovals, sprinkle with sesame seeds, and bake as savoury biscuits for 12–15 minutes.

Take a ball about the size of a tennis ball, roll it between your hands into a sausage shape about 1.25cm in diameter, and cut into halves or quarters. Sprinkle with coarse salt and bake for 12–15 minutes. Serve as breadsticks.

Roll out into small ovals, top with shredded mozzarella, fresh herbs and slivered garlic, and bake as mini-pizzas for 12–15 minutes.

This is adapted from a Bukhara recipe in *A Blessing of Bread* by Maggie Glezer, a lovely book about Jewish bread cookery all over the world. The flatbreads make an excellent accompaniment to before-dinner drinks, or they can be eaten on the side with a lunch of cold vegetable dishes and salads.

nooni tokhi

300ml water
60ml vegetable oil, plus
  extra for greasing
150g strong wholemeal
  bread flour
350g strong white bread
  flour
1 teaspoon cumin seeds
1 teaspoon salt
½ teaspoon fast-acting
  yeast

Put all the ingredients in the bucket following the order given in your manufacturer's instructions, or in the order listed here. Set the machine for the Knead/Dough setting. When the dough is ready, remove it to a floured work surface. Set the racks in your oven to the middle and upper levels and have ready two non-stick or lightly oiled baking sheets. Preheat the oven to 180°C/160°C fan/Gas 4.

Divide the dough into 12 pieces and roll each piece out into a circle 20cm in diameter. Put each circle on a baking sheet, and repeat until you have used all the available space. Prick the circles all over with a fork so that the crackers don't puff up too much in the oven. Bake until crisp (about 15 minutes). Cool on a wire rack.

Note: you can also use smaller pieces, about the size of a golf ball, and roll them out into 10cm circles. You don't need to prick them if you don't want to; they will expand to form a hollow balloon of crisp dough. The crackers will keep, tightly sealed, for several days if you are not using them all at once.

From *Nose to Tail Eating* by Fergus Henderson, a wonderful cookbook by the eminent restaurateur of St John, London EC1. You can make half the quantity if you're not serving these delectable pre-dinner nibbles to a large crowd, but the dough keeps well in the fridge for several days. This makes around 50 crackers, or a smaller number if you want to use them as flatbreads. And note: cumin and fennel seeds would also work well.

st john's crackers

125ml water
300g strong white bread flour
¾ tablespoon baking powder
½ teaspoon poppy seeds
½ teaspoon dill seeds
½ teaspoon caraway seeds
1 teaspoon salt
2 tablespoons extra virgin olive oil, plus extra for greasing

Put all the ingredients in the bucket following the order given in your manufacturer's instructions, or in the order listed here. Set the machine for the Knead/Dough setting. The dough can now be used immediately or left, covered in the fridge, if that suits you better. If you're not using it immediately, turn out into a lightly oiled bowl, turn once to coat with oil, cover with cling film, and leave until it has roughly doubled in size.

Preheat the oven to 220°C/200°C fan/Gas 7. Pinch off a piece of dough about the size of a large marble (30g) and roll it out on a floured work surface to a diameter of about 5cm. Place on a non-stick or greased baking sheet and roll out the remainder of the dough in the same way – or just use as much as you need. Bake near the top of the oven for 5 minutes, or until the crackers are crisp and lightly browned. Do not overcook or they will be too fragile. Transfer to a wire rack. Eat hot or at room temperature.

To make flatbreads: use pieces weighing about 100g and roll out into circles 12.5–15cm in diameter. Cook in the same way as the crackers.

Makes eight large buns or sixteen small ones. If you like, you can make a simple icing from icing sugar and water or milk to decorate the buns.

alice's raisin buns

For the dough
325ml milk
400g strong white bread
  flour
100g strong wholemeal
  flour
40g granulated sugar
50g muscovado sugar
50g butter
1 teaspoon salt
1½ teaspoons fast-acting
  yeast
oil, for greasing

For the filling
150g raisins
75g Brazil nuts, coarsely
  chopped
1 teaspoon cardamom
  seeds
1 teaspoon ground
  cinnamon
grated zest of 1 lemon
15g caster sugar
10g muscovado sugar
beaten egg, for brushing
icing sugar, for icing
  (optional)

Put all the dough ingredients in the bucket following the order given in your manufacturer's instructions, or in the order listed here. Set the machine for the Knead/Dough setting. In the meantime, combine the filling ingredients in a large bowl and mix together well.

Remove the kneaded dough to the bowl with the filling ingredients and mix the dough and filling together by turning and kneading. It will take a few minutes to get the filling distributed evenly.

Divide the dough into eight or sixteen pieces and form into balls which are round but slightly flattened – as if you were forming patties for hamburgers. Put them on a lightly oiled baking sheet, cover with cling film, and leave for 30 minutes or until the buns have roughly doubled in size.

Preheat the oven to 200°C/180°C fan/Gas 6. Put the baking sheet in the centre of the oven and bake for 15 minutes, or until they're nicely risen and well browned. Serve warm.

cakes and sweet loaves

My experience of bread machines has taught me that they should probably be called cake machines. The cakes that come out of them are just great, and they're little more trouble to make than bread. You don't get something round, of course, and you are limited in the size of what you can make. But just cut slices instead of wedges if you prefer, or slim wedges cut across the width of the cake-loaf. The appearance won't bother you once you take a taste. I promise.

This teatime favourite works very well in the bread machine, and in several different ways. Adding the larger quantity of yeast in this recipe gives a large and airy loaf, like 'regular' bread but with those delicious malt-loaf flavours. Using the lower quantity gives something closer to the traditional malt loaf: dense, compact, and ever so slightly gooey. Spread with butter (or clotted cream) and drink with best Ceylon or Assam tea. If you like, you can substitute sultanas or dried currants for the raisins. You can also use a combination of sugars and increase the quantity of malt extract by 50 per cent if you want more of that inimitable flavour. Some cooks like to brush the baked loaf (after cooling) with a glaze of honey or golden syrup.

malt loaf

300ml water
200g strong white
  bread flour
200g strong wholemeal
  bread flour
75g soft brown or
  muscovado sugar
75g butter, cut into
  small pieces
30ml malt extract
1 teaspoon salt
1–1¼ teaspoons fast-
  acting yeast
125g raisins

Put all the ingredients, except the raisins, in the bucket following the order given in your manufacturer's instructions, or in the order listed here. Add 50g of the raisins. Set the machine for the Basic/Raisin setting and medium loaf size, and set the Crust/Colour setting for medium. When the ping for adding ingredients goes off, or halfway through kneading, add the remaining raisins. Turn the loaf out onto a wire rack as soon as possible after baking is complete. Cool for at least 10 minutes before slicing – if you can resist the temptation.

A rich, dense bread that toasts up well. If you don't like chestnuts, walnuts can be used instead. The texture won't be the same, because the starch in chestnuts breaks up more readily than that of walnuts, but the flavour will be excellent. Spread slices of this unusual loaf with butter, or top with a sharp cheese such as mature Cheddar, Manchego, or something blue.

sweet chestnut bread

1 small onion, roughly chopped
1 tablespoon vegetable oil
¼ teaspoon herbes de Provence or another herb mixture
salt and freshly ground black pepper

For the dough
200ml milk
100ml water
100g self-raising flour
250g strong white bread flour
100g semolina
200g cooked chestnuts, roughly chopped
50g brown sugar
50g butter, cut into small pieces
1 teaspoon salt
1 teaspoon fast-acting yeast

Put the onion, vegetable oil and herbs in a small pan with a good dose of salt and freshly ground black pepper. Cook over a low heat, with regular stirring, just long enough to soften them lightly (5–10 minutes). Leave to cool.

Put all the dough ingredients in the bucket following the order given in your manufacturer's instructions, or in the order listed here. Add the onion mixture. Set the machine for the Basic setting and medium loaf size, and set the Crust/Colour setting for medium or high. Turn the loaf out onto a wire rack as soon as possible after baking is complete.

This soft, dense little number makes a satisfying but not insanely calorific dessert, especially good after lunch. Serve with crème fraîche or clotted cream if you like – though I don't find it necessary. Another note: don't try to slice this too thinly, the texture won't allow it.

squidgy banana cake

250g plain flour
2 teaspoons baking powder
1 egg
100g butter, melted
200ml milk
100g brown granulated sugar
1 teaspoon ground cinnamon
2 ripe bananas, mashed roughly with a fork

Remove the paddle from the bucket. Mix all the ingredients in a mixing bowl and spoon into the bucket. Bake using the Bake setting for 1 hour. Lift the bucket out of the machine, but leave the cake in the bucket for 10 minutes, then turn out carefully onto a wire rack. Turn the cake over and leave for at least 5 minutes before slicing.

For this loaf, the bananas should be as ripe as possible – and better still, over-ripe for maximum sweetness. This is really a dessert-bread, but a slice at breakfast with juice and coffee would start the day with a smile.

banana bread
the sweet stuff

300ml milk
400g strong white
  bread flour
100g butter, cut into
  small pieces
75g brown sugar
2 eggs
3 bananas, the riper
  the better, roughly
  chopped
1 teaspoon fast-acting
  yeast
1 teaspoon salt

Put all the ingredients in the bucket following the order given in your manufacturer's instructions, or in the order listed here. Set the machine for the Basic setting and medium loaf size, and set the Crust/Colour setting for medium. Turn the loaf out onto a wire rack as soon as possible after baking is complete.

The interior of this cake, with swirls of chocolate running through the sponge, is a sight for sore eyes. Again, it isn't overly sweet – you can add another 50g of sugar if you wish. As in any chocolate recipe, the key to success is using a really good dark chocolate with at least 60 per cent cocoa solids and preferably 70 per cent or above. Some would prefer to strain all the chunks out of the marmalade before baking, for a smoother result, but this is wasteful (you need to use at least an extra tablespoon) and makes for a less interesting texture.

chocolate marmalade marble cake

75g dark chocolate
175g butter, well softened and cut into small pieces
50g caster sugar
25g soft brown sugar
100g orange marmalade, not too chunky (this is 3 rounded tablespoons)
3 eggs
1 teaspoon baking powder
100g self-raising flour

Melt the chocolate in a heatproof bowl over a pan of gently simmering water. Cream the butter and sugars until the mixture is creamy and pale. Now add the marmalade and mix in, then add the eggs and mix again. Finally, add the baking powder and then the flour, a little at a time, and beat until smooth.

Scrape the chocolate into the bowl and stir in quickly; you don't need to mix it in completely because you want that lovely marbled effect. Remove the paddle from the bucket. Scrape the mixture into the bucket, smooth out the top, and bake using the Bake setting for 1 hour. Lift the bucket out of the machine, but leave the cake in the bucket for 10 minutes, then turn out carefully onto a wire rack. Turn the cake over and leave for at least 5 minutes before slicing.

The cake goes well with a scoop of vanilla ice cream.

This moist, tasty cake – given an unexpected lift by the coriander – wins over even the hearts of those who are not inclined by nature to love cake. It may be the best thing I've ever baked in the breadmaker.

squidgy carrot and coriander cake

300g self-raising flour
2 teaspoons baking powder
125g granulated sugar
3 small carrots (about 225g total weight), coarsely grated
1 teaspoon ground cinnamon
small handful fresh coriander, finely chopped
3 eggs, lightly beaten
250ml milk
125g butter, melted

Sift the flour and baking powder into a large bowl and stir in the sugar, carrots, cinnamon and coriander. Add the eggs, milk and butter, and mix quickly but thoroughly.

Remove the paddle from the bucket. Scrape the mixture into the bucket and cook using the Bake setting for 60–65 minutes. (Sixty minutes will give a really squidgy cake, so use the higher timing if maximum squidge is not to your liking.) Lift the bucket out of the machine, but leave the cake in the bucket for 10 minutes, then turn out carefully onto a wire rack. Turn the cake over and leave for at least 5 minutes before slicing.

If you like, you can make a simple cream cheese frosting to top this cake, as in the picture. Beat 50g cream cheese with 50g softened butter until smooth. Now gradually add 75–100g icing sugar until you have a smooth paste. Spread over the cake top and sprinkle on some chopped nuts if you want.

You could also try this with the juice from a pair of limes (but using the zest from just one of them) instead of lemon. The effect will be more delicate and very fragrant. The ideal beverage is a cup of tea, one of those designed for drinking without milk – Earl Grey, if you like it, or a delicate Darjeeling.

lemon and hazelnut cake

grated zest and juice of
1 unwaxed lemon
2 eggs, beaten
100g butter, melted
250g plain flour
2 teaspoons baking
powder
100g caster sugar
175ml semi-skimmed
milk
100g slivered hazelnuts

Mix the lemon zest and juice, eggs, butter, flour, baking powder, sugar and milk, plus half the hazelnuts, in a mixing bowl. Remove the paddle from the bucket. Spoon the mixture into the bucket. Scatter the remaining hazelnuts on top and press them into the batter so that most are submerged. Bake using the Bake setting for 1 hour. Lift the bucket out of the machine, but leave the cake in the bucket for 10 minutes, then turn out carefully onto a wire rack. Turn the cake over and leave for at least 5 minutes before slicing.

Roz Denny is one of the best cookery writers around, and a baking expert. This is my machine adaptation of her take on a simple drizzle cake.

roz denny's lemon drizzle cake

grated zest and juice of
  1 large unwaxed lemon
150g softened butter
150g golden caster sugar
2 eggs
150g self-raising flour
4 tablespoons milk
75g icing sugar, sifted

Put the lemon zest, butter, sugar, eggs, flour and milk into a large mixing bowl and beat using a wooden spoon or electric whisk until you have a smooth thick batter. Scrape down the side of the bowl once or twice during beating.

Remove the paddle from the bucket. Scrape the dough into the bucket and smooth out the top as best you can. Cook using the Bake setting for 40–50 minutes until the cake is well risen, golden brown on top and firm when pressed. You may also like to check it is cooked by piercing the centre with a thin skewer, which should come out clean. Lift the bucket out of the machine, but leave the cake in the bucket for 10 minutes, then turn out carefully onto a wire rack. Poke skewer holes in the top of the loaf as it cools.

Mix 1 tablespoon lemon juice and a splash of hot water with 25g of the icing sugar to make a thin syrup. Spoon this over the top of the cake so that it sinks in, then leave to cool completely.

When the cake is cold, mix the remaining lemon juice and icing sugar to make a smooth runny icing that holds its shape. Drizzle over the cake using a teaspoon or piping nozzle, allow to set, and serve in slices.

This makes a cake that is gooey and luscious but not overwhelmingly sweet. That's the way I like it, but many would want it sweeter. If you are one of them, use an extra 25–50g of sugar. Important note: add the berries straight from the freezer but separated from each other. If you have the good fortune to be baking this with fresh berries, chill them well before adding to the machine. Needless to say, this can be made with just one type of berry if you wish. My top choice would be blueberry, with raspberry running in a close second. If you want to make sure there's some berry on top, hold back a handful and drop it on just before you start the baking.

mixed berry cake

275g plain flour
2 teaspoons baking
    powder
100g caster sugar
250ml water
1 egg
100g butter, melted
150g frozen mixed
    berries

Remove the paddle from the bucket. Mix the flour, baking powder and sugar in a large bowl, then add the water, egg and butter, and blend thoroughly. Mix in the berries quickly, and scrape the mixture into the bucket. Smooth out the top. Bake using the Bake setting for 1 hour. Test by inserting a skewer into the centre; if it comes out hot and dry, the cake is done. If not, cook for another 10–15 minutes. Lift the bucket out of the machine, but leave the cake in the bucket for 10 minutes, then turn out carefully onto a wire rack. Turn the cake over and leave for at least 5 minutes before slicing.

If you like, you can serve this with a dollop of crème fraîche or clotted cream.

A fairly straightforward chocolate cake, but one that isn't nearly as sweet as some – just the way I like it. Add another 25g of sugar if you like it sweeter, and serve with vanilla ice cream if you're so inclined.

chocolate chip cake

250g plain flour
2 teaspoons baking
   powder
100g caster sugar
grated zest from ½ small
   orange
1 egg, beaten
100g butter, melted
200ml semi-skimmed
   milk
100g dark chocolate,
   cut into small pieces

Remove the paddle from the bucket. Mix all the ingredients, except the chocolate, in a mixing bowl and spoon into the bucket. Scatter the chocolate pieces on top and press them into the batter so that most are submerged. Bake using the Bake setting for 1 hour. Lift the bucket out of the machine, but leave the cake in the bucket for 10 minutes, then turn out carefully onto a wire rack. Turn the cake over and leave for at least 5 minutes before slicing.

Devised by my daughter Rebecca in a moment of reckless inspiration. A study in the *New England Journal of Medicine* has found that a daily slice of this cake will lead to permanent weight loss as long as you eliminate everything else from your diet except water and cucumbers.

triple chocolate cake

1 egg, beaten
125g butter, melted
250g plain flour
2 teaspoons baking
   powder
125g caster sugar
200ml semi-skimmed
   milk
50g each dark chocolate,
   milk chocolate and
   white chocolate, cut
   into small pieces and
   mixed together

Mix the egg, butter, flour, baking powder and sugar in a mixing bowl. Stir in the milk to blend, then quickly stir in half the chocolate pieces. Remove the paddle from the bucket. Spoon the mixture into the bucket. Scatter the remaining chocolate pieces on top and press them into the batter so that most are submerged. Bake using the Bake setting for 50 minutes. Test by inserting a skewer into the centre. If the skewer isn't hot and dry when it comes out, bake for another 5–10 minutes. Lift the bucket out of the machine, but leave the cake in the bucket for 10 minutes, then turn out carefully onto a wire rack. Turn the cake over and leave for at least 5 minutes before slicing. Take great care in turning out so you don't harm the still-soft network of chocolate pieces sitting on top.

When I was a child, the family dachshund climbed up onto the dining room table while we were washing dishes after a birthday dinner. Target: a half-eaten coconut cake. Mission: accomplished. I like to think that this moist and delicate cake would have been just as tempting for the hungry hound, who spent the next 24 hours lying semi-comatose on the living room floor.

coconut cake

300g self-raising flour
2 teaspoons baking
  powder
100g granulated sugar
2 teaspoons desiccated
  coconut
juice of 1 orange
1 egg, lightly beaten
100g butter, melted
250ml coconut milk

Sift the flour and baking powder into a large bowl and stir in the sugar and coconut. Add the orange juice, egg, butter and coconut milk, and mix quickly but thoroughly.

Remove the paddle from the bucket. Scrape the mixture into the bucket. Bake using the Bake setting for 50–60 minutes. (50 minutes will give a really squidgy cake, so use the higher timing if maximum squidge is not to your liking.) Lift the bucket out of the machine, but leave the cake in the bucket for 10 minutes, then turn out onto a wire rack. Turn the cake over and leave for at least 5 minutes before slicing.

Unusual, but definitely delicious. If you can't get the cordial, use all milk. It won't taste like the limed version, but it will still be good – those pineapple pieces are perfect for baking.

pineapple and lime cordial cake

100g butter
100g caster sugar
1 egg, beaten
250g self-raising flour
2 teaspoons baking powder
125ml semi-skimmed milk
100ml Rose's Lime Cordial
75g dried, sweetened pineapple pieces

Cream the butter and sugar in a large bowl until very well blended, then add the egg and beat until pale and airy. Add all the remaining ingredients and mix together thoroughly. Remove the paddle from the bucket. Spoon the mixture into the bucket. Bake using the Bake setting for 50 minutes, or until the top is lightly browned; it may take another 5 or 10 minutes. Lift the bucket out of the machine, but leave the cake in the bucket for 10 minutes, then turn out carefully onto a wire rack. Turn the cake over and leave for at least 5 minutes before slicing.

This recipe is based on one in Mireille Johnston's *French Cookery Course: Part One.* The late and greatly lamented Ms Johnston puts candied orange peel in her loaf. I would rather eat compost than candied peel, so I have left it out. If you don't share my aversion, add 2 tablespoons along with the lemon peel, etc. Mireille Johnston recommends serving this with poached peaches or pears. Who am I to argue?

pain d'épices

225g (about 100ml) clear honey
125ml water
2 teaspoons aniseed
1 teaspoon coriander
½ teaspoon ground cloves
1 teaspoon grated nutmeg
125g self-raising flour
175g rye flour
grated zest and juice of 1 unwaxed lemon
2 teaspoons baking powder
2 eggs, beaten
25g butter, melted

Mix the honey and water in a jug, heating the mixture slightly if they do not blend thoroughly. Put the aniseed and coriander in a mortar and pound with a pestle until coarsely ground. Add the other spices to the mortar.

Put the flours in a mixing bowl and add the spices and lemon. Pour in the honey–water mixture and stir to blend completely. Cover the bowl and chill for 2 hours (or even more) so that the flavours can develop.

Add the baking powder and the eggs, and stir well to mix completely. Remove the paddle from the bucket. Pour the mixture into the bucket and bake using the Bake setting for 65–70 minutes. Test by inserting a skewer into the centre. When it comes out hot and dry, the *pain* is done. Lift the bucket out of the machine, but leave the cake in the bucket for 10 minutes, then turn out carefully onto a wire rack. Turn the cake over and leave for at least 5 minutes before slicing.

The pears on top take on a nice colour and crisp up a little bit. Comice and conference pears both work, though comice has the edge. They don't need to be ultra-ripe, but they should be something short of diamond-hard. Vanilla ice cream, Greek yoghurt or crème fraîche would all partner well.

pear cake

150g butter, softened
100g golden granulated or caster sugar
2 eggs, lightly beaten
225g self-raising flour
1 teaspoon baking powder
½ teaspoon ground cinnamon
½ teaspoon vanilla extract
2 tablespoons milk
2 small, ripe pears
melted butter, for brushing

Put all the ingredients, except the pears, in a mixing bowl and beat with an electric whisk until smooth and creamy. Remove the paddle from the bucket. Scrape the batter into the bucket and smooth down the top.

Peel, core and quarter the pears lengthways. Lay them on top of the cake batter and bake using the Bake setting for 1 hour. Leave in the machine, uncovered, for 5–10 minutes before turning out. And take care when turning out that you don't tear, score, or otherwise damage the pears on top. Turn the cake over and leave for at least 5 minutes before slicing.

Simple, straightforward, delicious. As always where apples are concerned, a dose of cinnamon (about ½ teaspoon) and nutmeg would not go amiss here.

apple cake

275g self-raising flour
2 teaspoons baking powder
100g sugar
1 egg
200ml milk
100g butter, melted, plus extra for brushing
2 small eating apples, about 125g total weight

Sift the flour and baking powder into a mixing bowl and add the sugar. In another bowl, beat the egg with the milk and the melted butter.

Peel and core the apples, then cut off eight neat slices. Chop the rest into fairly large dice and mix with the egg–milk mixture. Remove the paddle from the bucket. Now place four slices of apple at the bottom of the bucket. Pour in the batter and top with the remaining four apple slices. Brush the slices with butter. Bake using the Bake setting for 1 hour. Lift the bucket out of the machine, but leave the cake for 10 minutes before turning out. This goes well with a scoop of vanilla ice cream on the side.

This really is halfway between cake and bread. Dense, sticky and sweet. If cooked for the longer time, this will be firmer and therefore easier to slice. I like it both ways, but marginally prefer the firmer version. This deeply flavourful item needs no accompaniment except a glass of milk or a cup of coffee.

maple and ginger cakebread

75g granulated golden
   sugar
100ml maple syrup
125g butter
225g self-raising flour
2 teaspoons bicarbonate
   of soda
1 teaspoon dried ginger
1 teaspoon finely
   chopped fresh root
   ginger
1 teaspoon ground
   cinnamon
2 eggs
250ml milk

Put the sugar in a small pan with 50ml of water. Heat slowly until the sugar has dissolved and deepened in colour slightly. Turn off the heat and add the maple syrup and butter, and leave the butter to melt.

Sift the flour, bicarbonate of soda, ginger (dried and fresh) and cinnamon into a mixing bowl. Beat the eggs with the milk and add to the bowl, mixing quickly, then add the sugar–butter mixture. Stir and fold well to blend all the ingredients thoroughly. Remove the paddle from the bucket. Scrape the batter into the bucket.

Bake using the Bake setting for 50 minutes, if you like a very gooey consistency, 60 minutes if you prefer it firmer and fully set. Lift the bucket out of the machine, but leave the cake in the bucket for 10 minutes, then turn out carefully onto a wire rack. Turn the cake over and leave for at least 5 minutes before slicing.

something unexpected

While fiddling around with the recipes in this brief chapter, I often found myself humming the George and Ira Gershwin song 'They All Laughed' (1937). These breadmaker recipes are not bread at all. But the bread machine can be viewed as something like a cross between an oven and a crockpot. So why not use it for things that are neither bread nor cake? These recipes are the result of my fiddling, and they're all really good. They give you something to do with the machine apart from baking, thus letting you get more for your initial outlay. The soupy and minced-meat possibilities are just about endless. Do your own fiddling and you'll make some good discoveries of your own, I promise. But note: after cooking all the recipes except the polenta, the bucket will need a proper cleaning.

When I fed tastes of this to a number of people, I didn't say I had cooked it in the bread machine. And they were shocked to discover the truth. But why should they have been? A loaf is a loaf, as far as the bread machine is concerned. Serve with just about any nice savoury bread, or home in on the Potato and Dill Bread on page 41.

meatloaf

serves 6–8

750g minced beef or lamb

2 streaky bacon rashers, rinds removed, finely chopped

1 medium onion, about 150g in weight, finely chopped

1 small carrot, finely chopped

1 celery stick, finely chopped

250g cooked rice or fresh breadcrumbs

small handful parsley, finely chopped

¼ teaspoon dried tarragon

¼ teaspoon dried oregano

¼ teaspoon dried sage

2 tablespoons vegetable oil

2 eggs, lightly beaten

2–3 tablespoons tomato ketchup (optional)

Mix all the ingredients, except the ketchup, in a mixing bowl. Remove the paddle from the bucket. Scrape one quarter of the mix into the bucket and pack down well, making sure that it fills out the corners. Add the remainder, level it out flat, and smooth down the top as best you can. Bake using the Bake setting for 75–80 minutes. The best way to test it if cooked is with an instant-read meat thermometer: stick it into the centre of the loaf and remove the loaf when the temperature reaches 68°C (155°F). If you don't have an instant-read meat thermometer, just stick in a metal skewer. When it comes away clean, hot and dry, the meatloaf is done. Lift the bucket out of the machine, but leave the loaf in the bucket for 10 minutes before turning out.

If you are turning out the loaf while it is hot, begin by draining the juices into a bowl: just tip up the bucket, holding the loaf in place so that it doesn't slip out. Then take great care turning out the loaf onto the serving plate, making sure that it doesn't slide out too quickly: heavy impact on the plate can cause the loaf to break up.

Just before serving, spread the top with ketchup, if you wish. It isn't really needed for flavour, but it adds a little bit of colour. Thinly sliced tomatoes or grilled peppers would also do the trick.

If you have access to minced veal, which is a good way to eat veal if you can't afford the expensive cuts, this is a very tasty dish. Do note, however, that it can also be made with minced pork (as long as it is lean enough) or minced chicken. Note: here's a way of using up stale bread! Note also: this is a low-cal specimen by meatloaf/terrine standards.

veal, herb and mustard loaf

serves 6–8

75g stale white or brown bread, cut into cubes or crumbs
100ml milk
650g minced veal (or pork or chicken)
2 medium onions, about 275g total weight
6–8 fresh mint, tarragon, or sage sprigs, or plain old parsley, chopped
1 tablespoon dry white wine
1 tablespoon Dijon mustard
1 tablespoon vegetable oil

Put the bread and milk in a small bowl and let them sit together, with occasional stirring, until the bread is pretty uniformly softened.

Mix all the ingredients in a mixing bowl. Remove the paddle from the bucket. Scrape one quarter of the mix into the bucket of your machine and pack down well, making sure it fills out the corners. Add the remainder, level it out flat, and smooth down the top as best you can. Bake using the Bake setting for 75–80 minutes. The best way to test it is cooked is with an instant-read meat thermometer: stick it into the centre of the loaf and remove the loaf when the temperature reaches 68°C (155°F). If you don't have an instant-read meat thermometer, just stick in a metal skewer. When it comes away clean, hot and dry, the meatloaf is done. Lift the bucket out of the machine, but leave the loaf in the bucket for 10 minutes before turning out.

If you are turning out the loaf while it is hot, begin by draining the juices into a bowl: just tip up the bucket, holding the loaf in place so that it doesn't slip out. Then take great care turning out the loaf onto the serving plate, making sure that it doesn't slide out too quickly: heavy impact on the plate can cause the loaf to break up.

One thing I really like about this soup is the flexibility of the timing. It's done after an hour and fifteen minutes but can go on cooking for another twenty or so without coming to any harm – and the longer time is good if you want the vegetables to be squishy-soft. Serve with a fairly simple bread, such as the Buckwheat Bread on page 27. This serves two to three, but the quantities can be increased by 50 per cent if you need to serve more.

butternut squash soup with pesto

serves 2–3

1 small butternut squash (about 350g in weight), peeled, de-seeded and coarsely chopped
2 large onions, about 350g total weight, coarsely chopped
4 plump garlic cloves, coarsely chopped
2 teaspoons vegetable oil
½ teaspoon herbes de Provence or another herb mixture
1 litre chicken or vegetable stock
small handful parsley, finely chopped
about 1 tablespoon extra virgin olive oil
about 1 tablespoon pesto
freshly grated Parmesan, for serving

Remove the paddle from the bucket. Put the squash, onions, garlic, vegetable oil, herbs and stock in the bucket. Cook using the Bake setting for 75 minutes. Stir once or twice, especially in the last 30 minutes of cooking. Taste a piece of squash to see if it is soft enough. If you want it to be softer, give it up to 20 minutes more. If it suits your schedule, you can leave the cooked soup sitting in the machine for a good 20 minutes longer – it retains its heat well.

When you're ready to serve, divide the soup between the bowls and sprinkle the parsley on top. Drizzle a little extra virgin olive oil on each one, then plop on a blob of pesto. Serve immediately with the cheese passed separately.

Seasonings can be varied endlessly; those here are nothing more than a suggestion. And if you feel like it, you can jazz up the soup by passing around chutneys, relishes or pickles.

chicken soup with rice

serves 4 as a starter

100g (around 50ml) long grain rice
1 litre chicken or vegetable stock
2 celery sticks, thinly sliced
2 plump garlic cloves, finely chopped
2 shallots, finely chopped
½ teaspoon dried tarragon
a good knob of butter
100g skinless and boneless chicken, thinly sliced
small handful parsley or fresh dill, finely chopped

Soak the rice in cold water to cover for 20 minutes, then rinse and drain well. Remove the paddle from the bucket.

Put all the ingredients, except the chicken and fresh herbs, in the bucket. Cook using the Bake setting for 1 hour. Stir once or twice, especially in the last 30 minutes of cooking.

Taste a few grains of rice; if they are not fully cooked, continue cooking for as long as you need to get them nice and soft (5–10 minutes more).

When the rice is cooked, add the chicken pieces. Stir well and continue cooking until the chicken is just done – 5 or 10 minutes should do the trick. Serve with the fresh herbs sprinkled on top.

Polenta cooked in the bread machine needs less attention than when it is cooked in a pan. I'm pretty sure this is because the heat comes from all sides rather than just from the bottom, but whatever the reason, it's a nice discovery. Note the procedure for making firm polenta, the kind you leave to cool and then slice for grilling, frying or baking. And remember to use a non-metallic spoon for stirring, as metal might scratch the bucket's non-stick coating.

polenta

serves 4–6
  as a side dish

125g coarse polenta
  (cornmeal)
850ml water
1 teaspoon salt
2 tablespoons extra
  virgin olive oil
freshly grated Parmesan,
  (optional), for serving

Remove the paddle from the bucket. Put all the ingredients, except the oil, in the bucket and give them a good stir. Cook using the Bake setting for 40 minutes. You don't need to stir often – three or four times will do the trick – but you can stir and check a few more times if that suits you. The polenta is done when it is soft and creamy. Stir in the oil and serve immediately with freshly grated Parmesan, if you like.

For firm polenta, cook for an extra 5 minutes. Stir in the oil thoroughly. Lift the bucket out of the machine and leave until the polenta has set and cooled completely. Turn out of the bucket onto a chopping board. Chill it, covered, if you are going to be storing it for more than 30 minutes. To serve, cut into slices and grill or fry until well browned on both sides.

index

acknowledgements

First thanks to everyone at Kyle Cathie Books, the best publisher any cookery writer could ask for. Special thanks there to my editors, Jennifer Wheatley and Catharine Robertson.

This book looks beautiful because of Will Heap, who took the photographs; Annie Rigg and Rachel Wood, who did the cooking and food styling; Sue Rowlands, who styled the props; and Mark Latter, who designed the book. My heartfelt and humble thanks to all of them.

Special thanks to various people for advice and help of different sorts. Bryony Allen lent me her bread machine at a time when I was testing recipes, thus speeding up the work greatly. Roz Denny, Fran Warde, Sally Cox, Sue Lawrence and John and Mary Whiting either lent me recipes or exchanged views. Numerous readers of the *Guardian* and *Independent on Sunday* wrote to me with views on bread machines which helped me modify my misguided prejudices.

As always, I thank my wife, Emma Dally, and my daughters, Rebecca, Alice and Ruth. In addition to tasting the fruits of my labours, they made useful suggestions and – in the case of Rebecca and Alice – helped me test recipes and came up with some recipes of their own.

Finally I thank my Green Johanna composter (www.greatgreensystems.com). During the testing of recipes for this book, Johanna swallowed many dozens of kilos of bread that I was not able to eat or give away. And she never complained.